LIGHT YEARS

New and
Selected Poems
by DABNEY STUART

Louisiana State University Press

Baton Rouge and London

1994

Designer: Glynnis Phoebe
Typeface: Centaur
Typesetter: G&S Typesetters, Inc.
Printer and binder: Thomson-Shore, Inc.

LIBRARY OF CONGRESS CATALOGING-IN-PUBLICATION DATA

Stuart, Dabney, date.
    Light years : new and selected poems / by Dabney Stuart.
        p.   cm.
    ISBN 0-8071-1898-2. — ISBN 0-8071-1899-0 (pbk.)
    I. Title.
    PS3569.T8L54   1994
    811'.54—dc20
                                          94-11453
                                          CIP

Poems herein have been selected from *The Diving Bell* (Alfred A. Knopf, 1966), copyright © 1964, 1965, 1966 by Dabney Stuart; *A Particular Place* (Alfred A. Knopf, 1969), copyright © 1965, 1966, 1968, 1969 by Dabney Stuart; *The Other Hand* (Louisiana State University Press, 1974), copyright © 1974 by Dabney Stuart; *Round and Round* (Louisiana State University Press, 1977), copyright © 1977 by Dabney Stuart; *Common Ground* (Louisiana State University Press, 1982), copyright © 1982 by Dabney Stuart; *Don't Look Back* (Louisiana State University Press, 1987), copyright © 1977, 1980, 1982, 1983, 1984, 1985, 1986, 1987 by Dabney Stuart; and *Narcissus Dreaming* (Louisiana State University Press, 1990), copyright © 1981, 1983, 1984, 1985, 1986, 1987, 1988, 1989, 1990 by Dabney Stuart. Grateful acknowledgment is made to the editors of publications in which poems in this volume previously appeared, some in slightly different form: *Balcones, Crazy Horse, Crescent Review, Denver Quarterly, Hampden-Sydney Poetry Review, Harvard Magazine, The Journal, Kenyon Review, Lillabulero, Malahat Review, Mediterranean Review, Memphis State Review, New Orleans Review, New Virginia Review, Oxford Magazine, Panhandler, Ploughshares, Poetry Miscellany, Poetry Northwest, Prairie Schooner, Red Clay Reader, Shenandoah, Southern Poetry Review, Southwest Review, Tar River Poetry, Tendril, Virginia Quarterly Review,* and *Zone 3.* "Hidden Meanings" is reprinted from *Massachusetts Review,* The Massachusetts Review, Inc. © 1985. "The River" originally appeared in *The New Yorker.* "The Midget," "The Student," "Sunburst," and "Ties" are from *Poetry,* and "Begging on North Main," "Gospel Singer," "High Wire," "Hunter, Prey," "Once More for My Lady," and "Taking the Wheel" from *Southern Review.* "Snorkeling in the Caribbean" first appeared in *Landscape and Distance: Contemporary Poets from Virginia* (University Press of Virginia, 1975). Of the new poems, "Leave-taking" appeared originally in *Chelsea;* "Sleepwalker," in *Chronicles;* "Coming To," in *Four Quarters;* "Love Poems," in *Kentucky Poetry Review;* "Love's Body," in *Sewanee Review;* "Light Years," in *Southern Poetry Review;* "Commencement," "Fence," and "The Writing Machine," in *Southern Review;* "Presence" and "Tending," in *Tar River Poetry;* "Percussion," in *TriQuarterly;* and "His Granddaughter Arrives," in *Virginia Quarterly Review.* "The Executive Discovers Poetry" was first published in *The Gettysburg Review* and is reprinted by permission. "The Funeral" originally appeared in *The New Yorker.* "The Water's Fine, I'm Fine" is from *The Southern California Anthology* (1991).

The author is grateful to Washington and Lee University for a Glenn Grant that helped him in the final stages of selection and arrangement of this volume.

Publication of this book has been supported by a grant from the National Endowment for the Arts in Washington, D.C., a federal agency.

for Sandra
and for the QM, Moley, and Wynne

CONTENTS

A PRAYER

Jonathan Swift, that scorpion,
Wrote *Gulliver,* and then grew pale
To find the venom in his tail
No longer served as medicine.

Stretched on the cutting table, he'd
Worn various masks for surgery,
Yet through the gauze, beyond the bone,
The face he'd seen had been his own;
He learned from practice the unsure
Distinction between disease and cure.

Though it killed him in the end
He was his own best doctor.
                                    Bless
His strain, Mnemosyne, and lend
Such healing distance to their bitterness.

The Warehouse Chute

As a boy I started at the top,
Sixth floor, as high as my father's business
Reached, a sort of skyline
In a squat and stolid city
Where men moved among goods, and knew
Themselves as the goods moved, always down.
But that was their concern
And none of my business.
Seated on cardboard or wax paper
I spiraled that metal slide
Past every merchandise
At jerkneck speed, and didn't care
If I never stopped, because
I knew I would—come to the smooth
Bright easy finish of that ride.

I never needed Virgil
Or thought of him, but now
That place seems hell enough—
A house of wares which never spoke
A word, or sang a song,
Yet held its men, my father
And his father, as a sorcerer
Enthralls a knight,
Benights an age, held them
And made them move
As it would have them move
In darkness and in circles
Wearing them empty as that chute—
Seems hell enough.
Now in my dreams the spiral
Spirals without end.

I see myself on every level
Smiled at by a carton,
Never Beatrice, smiled at
By this past that hands me on,
Guideless, always going down.

The Soup Jar

Its metal top refused my father's twisting;
He tried warm water, a dishcloth, the heel of a shoe,
But couldn't budge its stubborn *status quo.*
It had stood its ground, longer than he, rusting.

I had tried to help. Gripped the jar while he cursed
Into place the tricky gadget guaranteed
To open anything, then gave it all he had.
I jerked my hand, and a hunk of glass, back when it burst.

Someone else tied my tourniquet. He paled
And had to sit down. Seven stitches later
We cleaned the floor and had another dish for supper.
Alone, he got nothing. It took us both to fail.

Weeks after, my world spun around that jar
And I saw it, and him, through angry tears.
Now it seems, recalled through these shattered years,
So small a thing—some broken glass, a scar.

People Asleep

The houses are dark now. People asleep
In their separate lives during the day
Admit it doesn't matter and close their eyes.

My father, worn out with fishing, casts flies
In his dream pond, dark, but not dark in the way
That houses are dark now. The woman asleep

Beside him doesn't see how he lures the prize
Bass no one has hooked this summer. She'd say
What difference does it make? and close her eyes

On his quaint struggle. Why should she be surprised?
It's the selfsame bass he fights with every May.
Since houses are dark now and the woman asleep

In her separate dreams ignores the deep
Fish churning and the rod's taut play
That matters so much behind my father's eyes,

Who will hear at the netting when he cries
This is my catch. It never gets away.
Houses are dark now. People asleep
Admit it doesn't matter and close their eyes.

TIES

When I faded back to pass
Late in the game, as one
Who has been away some time
Fades back into memory,
My father, who had been nodding
At home by the radio,
Would wake, asking
My mother, who had not
Been listening, *What's the score?*
And she would answer *Tied,*
While the pass I threw
Hung high in the brilliant air
Beneath the dark, like a star.

A Garland for Marshall

for L. M. von Schilling (1874–1954)

Rescue

I have looked at this photograph
Of you at rest in that rowboat
For hours, but can't see your face.
When my eyes finally go slack
The dark space
Between your white shirt and hat
Becomes a hole in the bay
Behind you, and I fall in.
I am no better swimmer
Now than I was at five
And the past is more treacherous water
Than the creek you fished me from
Then, finding me by the bubbles
That were the chain of my breath.
Going down again, lifesaver,
Where it is darker and deeper,
I leave the same trail,
Believing that where you've been
Is the only depth I'll sound
That may save me for myself.

Last Words

For I am proverb'd with a grandsire phrase.

Ten miles out of Cherbourg, a blind ship broke the fog
And ripped your vessel's hull thirty feet aft
Of where you stood, watching the inert darkness wed the flood.
While the crew sealed off compartments, released life rafts
For the steerage, you chose the first-class lounge and tapped a keg.

In your name drank to something—death or fear?—as though your blood
Battened on hazard, took mishap at the swell.

G-men, checking every angle that First War,
Couldn't imagine you into subversion,
If anything cut themselves on your name,
Found their blood, as yours, was American,
For which neither you nor they were to blame.
Spies themselves, caught in some odd metaphor,
They taught you liberty's emblem was a cracked bell.

During Prohibition, your bootlegging cohort
Docked his freight at your wharf, crossed the yard
In broad daylight, tipsy, calling your name.
You dodged that tasteless law as though it were sport,
Knowing how an unpredictable game
Raises men's spirits most when they're off guard,
Knowing good blood improves bad alcohol.

These things I've been told, or read in your letters.
I remember other things firsthand—but most, your frame
Dwindled and racked by paralysis, sailing waters
For three wrecked years flat on your back, your words
Refined to five, as though new senses, or else strange surds
Life had reduced you to. You forgot your name
But your blood solved the last problem in its cells.
You cried *God damn it to hell,* voicefather. Straight to hell.

BREAKWATER

When the wooden sea guard
Before your house began to rot, the stakes
Of its support work loose from the soft slats,
And high tide leak into your yard,

You pulled out cement from your stow of tricks
And chucked the old planks to the water rats.

The man you hired to pour
The concrete worked
His trowel like a sculptor, though unmoved
By the force he shored
The land against, or what, to a landlocked
Aging man, the sea wall proved.

That shining wall's there yet, Grandfather,
Where you put it. I see it in my dreams
As a grin a man might grin before he cursed,
As you cursed on your deathbed at that Other
Who stove your seams.
I stand upon it now through every weather
Bearing your oath, for better or for worse.

The Widow

for Martha H. von Schilling (1884–1967)

At his grave ten years after
She fingers an azalea half covering the stone,
Says *It's double*, decides it's beautiful.
Removing two wild cherry shoots from the plot
She notices a rude vine
Wound to a large box trunk
And pulls it up, at its root.
The black earth crumbles like wake
Over her shoes. She kicks it
Off, toeing it back where it was.

At home, there's no one to keep her
Out of the bottom drawer, whose scrapbooks
Freeze for her what slips her mind:
His face among others, their
Children, honors, holidays;
But she remembers no voices,
No sunlit laughter from the girl
On the wharf, no music for the dance
No one is dancing. Nor is there movement
From the outstretched hand, or the bodice
Laced over the next breath.
It is very much like heaven, she thinks,
Where everything must grow for its silent joy
Being always simply a gesture of itself
And there is no memory, none at all.

She passes over
Two letters she has kept, written
Ten years after their wedding.
She knows that he jokes in one of them
He needs new calling cards

Telling who he is beyond his name:
Father, husband, plyer of a half dozen trades
And *Every kind of Damn Fool*
Known to man, but now doing original research;
That in the other he promises
It is absolutely settled he will
Never go away again alone.

A Gesture

for Carrie Haynes Stuart (1879–1951)

I remember you bowed,
Grandmother: over the stove
Tending the dough you leavened
Into bread; over the bed you made
Tucking the cornered sheets
Precisely under the mattress
You died on; over your husband
Kissing goodnight those lips
Which muttered the market page
Reports as you left the room;
And at grace before meals,
The words so much your own
They spoke themselves,
Blessing you.

As though life itself were a feast
You were obedient to
You bowed to it each time you moved,
Leavening us, giving rise
To a silent order we could dream
In the beds we made.
And here, tonight, cornered by distances
Husbands and wives expand
As they reach over,
I ask that you take my bow
Not to a name, but to your human grace.

Taking Sides

What holds the floor up, Father,
The money underneath? We bring each other
To this bank, walking on a need
Fragile as a thrush egg, the color of
This marble floor, remembering our seed
Which broke its violence quietly as a dove.

Our entrance separates us. In your aisle
A vacant distance holds your future wide
And clear. No fortitude or guile
Can bar you from that door. I'm inside,
Your teller for a change, odd guardian
Of what we've come here for, old loss and gain

Snared in columns since my grandfather
Founded this place. Following each other
We don't know where to stop. This wily maze
Of desks and records I wander like a fox
Become a hunter who may flush grace
But cannot tree your safe-deposit box.

You've got me looking backward. Up to now
I'd thought I was awake, our strain at peace
With its succession. But from the start
We've juggled the books of our own house.
Nobody's balanced them, or shows me how
To trick the answer caging us apart.

THE RIVER

The lifeguard's whistle organized our swimming
Around the anchored raft at summer camp,
Saving us from the tricky channel current.
When he blew it we gave in to the system,
Each raising his buddy's hand in the sudden quiet
To be reckoned, officially, among the living.
Half a pair meant someone might have drowned
Or, more likely, not checking out, gone back
To his cabin where no one made him buddy,
Where, if he wished, he could desert the raft,
The restricting whistle, all practiced safety,
And dreaming the channel's bottom, sound
That deep cut, the rocks' dark hollows, and the cold.

I have been back once, when no one was there,
And poked around in the empty cabins,
Boarded against vandals as if something valuable
Were left to steal, where no one was dreaming.
Yet, as if in a dream, I saw a name
The same as mine printed in faded chalk
On a wall, and I took a dented canteen
With a torn case from a nail rusted with rain.
It lay on the beach with my clothes while I went swimming
Where the channel cuts deep across from the steady raft,
Without a buddy. In over my head
I finned to the bottom, expelling breath
Until the cold pressure cracked in my ears,
Then fought that pressure upward with my arms
And shot, like a dolphin, high
Into the weightless air
Over and over again, each time higher,

Until I could use the bottom as a springboard.
However high I went, there was always bottom.

After, I took the canteen to the springs
Which feed the river, and filled it.
It hangs now on a nail in my room,
And when the season's dry and the city liquid
Tastes too much of metal and the system
That pumps it to my taps,
I drink that water, and find it cool and clear.

Two for Wynne

Birthday

Sister, you're ten today. Your first decade
Ends, as they all will, in the spring.
Your years, with the seasons, bring
You to the brightening of the spade,
Light's lengthening, the magic seed,
Sweet showers, and the earth's reopening.
Outside your window, jonquils thrust their need
In two directions for the blossoming.
It's just another day. For dancing school
You tighten up, pointing your toes
And arms, caught in the awkward pull
Toward grace. Fragile, maybe you'll grow
Enough to take that weight, and fool
Us all recital day. Who knows?

It doesn't bother you. You're hardly tired
When Yogi Bear postpones your dinner hour
With his preposterous ballet. No longer scared
Of the dark, you still fight bedtime, glower,
Perform extended goodnights for your father
Who, at sixty-six, has not retired.

Prokofiev and Peter whirl you off
To your sleep. Beside you, my once-
Upon-a-time follows your innocence
Out of this world. I keep what's left—
An even stranger Yogi, another wolf
You haven't dreamed of, and a dance
I'm bound to practice, gulf to gulf,
Done to the unschooled catch of circumstance.

Girl at Play

When your fingers squeeze the bulb
The mysterious air
You feed the toy dog on the sidewalk
At the other end of the tube
Swells and will not stay in
His tiny body.
When he hops and squeals
You jump as though at tube's end
Yourself, unable to contain
The press of breath.

In the background, across the street,
Your father, hands in pockets,
Stands among shadows. His eyes
Accept their secrets, receding
Into another distance, yet holding you
Fast and quiet where you move apart.

Canned Goods

My belly full of this domestic life
I stalk the kitchen, hungry for sharp knives.
Or poison. My cat, content with all nine lives,
Gets in his licks. I want to leave my wife,

To hit the alleys with him where he howls
The stupid moon, claws over garbage cans,
Toms every Tabby. The shrivel's in my glands:
I'm fixed. He goes alone. I move my bowels.

He'll come back in the morning for his milk,
Evaporated, chock full of goodness,
On the same shelf whose plentitude I bless
And lift a can from now. I'm of his ilk.

Sweet Life the label says. I wonder whose.
Inside the tin, where it's all over, peas
Dumbhuddle in their well-arranged repose.
Out here, I'm in the dark. I have to choose.

FIREWORKS

for my daughter

Sitting beside you in that rented city
I watched the fabulous lights
Flicker all over the walls and ceiling,
And had trouble telling
Them from the shadows they brought in.
You rode the double bed like a princess
In a dream, all but lost
In the hollow between the pillows.
You slept without a twitch
But I couldn't hear your breathing for the noise.

When it was over and your mother
Took my place I went outside
With echoes in my head, and your
Image burning in my eyes.
I found above me the same dark bowl
I swim in every night, year in year out,
Leaking a few old stars.

FLATFISH

I'll crush you, said sea.
I'll flatten, said flounder.

I'll make your eyes war.
I'll watch you, said flounder.

I'll muck up your color.
But not my scales, said flounder.

You'll eat slime.
I'll eat, said flounder.

You'll live on the bottom.
I'll live, said flounder.

Resignation, said sea.
Grace, said flounder.

from
A PARTICULAR PLACE
(1969)

Spring Song

This April some swelltoad begins again
His awkward run over the stones and mud
On the river's bottom he looks like,
Taking in
Through a mouth whose solid bone
Seems made to break stone
Whatever keeps him going. Though the hook
That smoothly takes another fish cannot crack
That mouth, he will be caught, will swell
On land into a perfect ball,
Defenseless as air,
And the fisherman will find
The meat inside as white
As milk, as sweet
To his mouth as to a mind
That has fed on mud and stones
A song can be, sung in the bones.

The Charles River

Cambridge:
From the Cowley Fathers Monastery

I

On Memorial Drive, outside the cloister wall
The sycamores peel: there a layer
Beneath a layer beneath
A layer of bark,
Hinting a way inside.

Though there are people inside
The cloister, I
Never saw a soul, and I
Used to walk often under those sycamores
Beside the river. The shadows
Cast by their limbs at night
Seemed the same as the shadows their limbs cast
By day—a shadow
Beneath a shadow, shadowed.

2

Faces would pass by me
Day and night: the mother
From the park, a student
Under the influence of Thoreau,
A clerk from the Coop, off duty,
The full professor whose eyes
Lay open like a book face down on a table.

If I were to dream one face
Approaching me under the sycamores
Beside the river, it would be

Her face beneath his face beneath
Her face. It would be
A manner of seeing
As a dream is, as a poem is
A manner of speaking,
A shadow, a way inside.

3

We walk there
Beside the river beneath the sycamores
Where others sit on their books
Reading the water the way a child
Watches its grandmother crochet a shawl.

Perhaps the people inside the cloister
Hear rumors of all this,
Watching from their casements
The water through the sycamores.
Perhaps all of us
Have looked at the river together
Sometime in our moving
Beneath the shadows of those trees
Darkening, and imagined
It would take us in.

BOSTON:
FROM THE EMBANKMENT

1

On summer evenings here
Lovers may kiss to Stravinsky:
Le sacre du printemps.
If they lie close enough
To the bank, the music and the river
Lapping the stones

Become one sound, one
Sound also with the beat
Of the ducks' wings flying
Above the lovers, the ducks' wings folding
As they settle in.

2

There is an instant, a point of turning
When a duck seems poised
On the tip of one wing, a point of
Turning before the settling in.
He seems to sail then,
His wing taking the air
As those white sails take it
Into themselves, filling,
Moving the shells over the water
With the swiftness of birds.

With the swiftness of fish
The shell moves under the water,
The fin of its sail filled,
Taut, still, yet moving, pointed down,
Its tip a point of turning.
The sail over the river, the sail
Beneath it, the wing of a duck's poise
Above it move the world
Moves on the point of its turning.

3

Behind my back, the streets
Can make everything
Seem a matter of names:
Brimmer, the filled glass—
The singing blossom, Chestnut, Spruce, and Lime—
An old warning, Revere,
And two chimes ringing—

Or, between me and the river,
The Union Boat Club,
Hatch Memorial Shell:
Matter and names, yolk and white
In the one shell, hatching

A manner of speaking
As a poem is, as a dream is
A manner of seeing

As the dream of a poem
Hears the one sound
The rites of spring beating their wings
Above the lovers, the music
Lapping the stones, the river
Kissing the down
Down of the ducks, coming in

Or as the poem
Imagines a wing
A white sail
A fin
And cannot tell
Whether the river reflects
The white wing beating
The sail rippling, or the air
Reflects the white sail rippling,
The deep fin beating,
And cannot tell
Which part of the one world
Watches itself, as Narcissus watched
Himself from the depth of his longing

And his loveliness until it took him in.

SUNBURST

A friend writes
How's the prince?
I bet he's a pisser.

He is.
Anywhere:
In his bath,
Naked under the sun,
Getting his pants changed—
The sudden burst
The rise
The high peak
And the fall.

Not a word
But this bow
Warm as spring rain,
Rainbow,
Pot of gold,
Dazzling
Curve of the world.
When he grows up
May he find
Such light
Such shape
Such perfect levity
For what he can't use.

1

This pencil moves on the page
White as a swan's quill,
Making its music
With no more noise than a swan
Makes moving
Over the rippling lake.

Three hundred years ago
Men wrote
With the feathers of birds,
And courtly fingers
Picked airs
From the lute with plectra
Made from the feathers of birds.

2

This pencil, Venus 2,
This unwieldy timber
You can start a fire with,
This shaving
That writes *tree*,
This small stick
That bears the name of a goddess
And can write *love*
As cleanly as a knife
Cuts the names of lovers
Into the bark of trees,
Leaves its marks on this white paper
With no more noise
Than a pebble
Thrown by two lovers

In late afternoon
Makes, sinking
Through the water
Of a lake, played on
By the shadows of trees.

3

The river in its narrows
Moves on over the stones,
Riffles, moves on over
The stones, reflects the sun,
Moves on, covering the stones
Played on by the shadows of trees.

A fisherman's rod
Moves through its arc, the fly
Settles on the water,
Drifts through the sun,
Plays in the shadows of trees,
Moves on over the stones
To the end of the line, jerks,
Drifts, jerks.
The fisherman's blood
Hums in its veins,
Moves on over his bones.

4

The small-mouth bass
Hovers over the pebbles
In the moving water,
Watching the fly jerk,
Drift, jerk.
Dappled, motionless
As a stone, he waits
On his hunger, and will rise
For the fly in one

Invisible swiftness,
As the fisherman's need
Rises silently to words
Through the depths of his dreams.

5

Scattered along the shore
Among the stones
Untouched by the water
The bones of birds
Lie, bleached whiter
Than this page, played on
By the shadows of trees.

6

Above the still lake water
And the moving stream,
Above their beds of stones,
The wings of birds
Make no more noise
Than this pencil moving
Across this page, leaving
Its weight of words,
Makes no more noise
Than the bass striking
The fly, no more
Than the fly drifting,
Jerking, drifting, no
More than the fisherman's need
Rising through his sleep
Leaving his dreams
Through words that seem
In their silence
To fly under the sun,
Nest in the shadows of trees.

Two for My Daughter

Confirmation

1 The World

Because of the way one thing
Blends with another,
It's hard to tell where the edges
Are, when
Winter ends and winter begins,
How close a star is,
How far it is to yourself,
How much you discover when you lose,
Like Columbus.

Be ready
To touch everything
Inside out.

2 The Flesh

You can touch with this
If you remember
It's not the only thing.

3 The Devil

Like God, he describes
The edges we are afraid of.
Each of us
In a different language

Must love him to death.

LINES

You sing in my lap
In your twilight sleep,
One finger nodding the tune
In the air while the train
Wheels hum and clack
To their beaten track.

When I was your singing age
A fireman earned his wage
Keeping the pressure up.
We're diesel and longer range
Now, for our yearly trip.
We move from stage to stage.

By night you've sung
Yourself awake.
You remind me of the trout
I caught which began our week,
And say it's wrong
To use live bait.

The lights by the rails slow down
As your mother waves
Us in. Through the train
Window I promise to save
You a week the next July.
You wave goodbye.

Goodbye. Now I'll go back
To the end of the line
Where I live, and learn
To tie
An artificial fly
Which hides the hook.

The Student

Under the rusting elms his separate path
Crossing and recrossing the separate paths
Of others like himself, whose aimless feet
Weave some invisible pattern on the grass,
Takes him to his classroom, to his seat,
Where he walks on words toward a drowning man
He dimly imagines, or pictures in vague dreams,
A shifty man whose face he thinks familiar
As his own, yet cannot fix exactly,
Who calls to him when he walks out again
Onto the solid earth to thread his way
Under the rusting elm leaves, which float down
Like nets through water seeking the vagrant school.

THE LEAF EATER

The wind-sacked beast
Chugs and whines across the campus lawn
Sucking up the leaves in ordered rows
Before the first freeze and the winter snows.
He watches from his office, stifles a yawn,
Thinks they have fallen for this raucous feast.

Since quitting time
Last night dogwood and elm did as they always do,
Dropping what was lifeless, coming clean,
While that machine
Cooled off in the shed, deflated and askew,
Hungover from its swinish pantomime.

But, again this morning, swollen like a sow,
It gorges on dead leaves, and its own noise,
So loud his thoughts go haywire. The childish
Fantasies he had cast off as trash
Heap up, tempting his windy hunger. A voice
Says *Eat*, and he fills the vacuum made by his old vow

To think austerely, dropping his green schemes.
Though dry at first, this fare
Suddenly turns sumptuous as spring
Beneath whose trees, ardent and flourishing,
The ghost of a boy turns cartwheels, unaware
He lives beyond the seasons of his dreams.

WE NEVER CLOSE

There is no substitute for mind.
You cannot wash it down, or off.
It works if you are dumb or blind,
Believes enough is not enough.

Mind decides and mind reneges,
Bares its designs in secret roots;
Drinks nothing up, yet leaves the dregs,
Tilts back its hat and draws, and shoots.

Fingers your navel, tickles your twat,
Lays you out flat but remains aloof,
Teaches the body it is not,
Offers itself its own disproof.

Makes pictures, but none of itself,
Watches the horse it rides go round,
Scrambles a box of childhood toys
Into tomorrow's lost and found.

Never forgets the holes it finds,
Wants justice, and then cops a plea;
Says to the creatures whom it binds
Undo yourself and set me free.

LOVE SONG

When I was dying
I held the lamp as high as my feet:

Looking down out of the darkness
I saw where I could walk,

Saw for the first time
How the path made its own way.

If I had waited a hundred times
Or until my feet froze to the light

I would have covered the same ground,
Met myself at the same edges,

Invented the same scraps
Of a dream I couldn't assemble.

I rustle among them now
Borne by the sound of my feet

Shuffling this puzzle, and the sound,
Distant, of someone scraping,

As though digging a well,
Burying a bone,

Planting a seed
In this troubled radiance.

High Wire

All the way he heard someone breathing.

It seemed he walked that breathing
As toward the source of a wind
Or a far voice echoing.

He looked back once—
The place where he began followed him.

I'm not getting anywhere he said
And saw he was closer.

He was the focus of distances;
He stood still and heard the same space
Balancing.

When I come to the end, he thought,
I will turn and say *Here,*

Take my hand.

from
THE OTHER HAND
(1974)

you kept
offering up
unbroken
however wide we spread it.
And nothing came true.

Nothing
kept coming true.

Urban Hunting Scenes

1
No one I meet is ever armed
but each morning I sharpen my thorns.

2
It's not as though there are beasts
either,
but I keep my threats poised,
like a net.

3
At noon
I send my shadow out beside me.

I teach it to flatten
against walls,
to balance on the split pavement,
to stalk.

At night in the dark
it cleaves to me.

4
Like frost
I fasten against the midnight
windows of beautiful women.

I can't tell them
from dreams.

Deer

Animal Forest Park, N.H.

their hesitant circling,
their precarious ribs,
their voices

           balked . . .

The sky lowered.

They lay down by a gate.
Their necks turned in the dust like keys.
Nothing
opened.

They stood up again.
They looked.
The fences in their eyes grew.
I turned away
thinking   *Everything*
diminishes
except loss.

Their eyes will break with it,
spilling through the barred distance
to you and me, their

keepers.

The Elect

They ascend into themselves
above the figures of shame
as a crow flees its shadow.

They angle toward noon.
Were the sun a needle
they would thread it with their steep pride
and sew *God* on the sky, their
sampler.

But all light,
waking,
shales from them;

if they could look down
they would see
the ground starred with it.

If they could return
they would congregate in the cedars
of winter, their locked eyes
the color of snow,

reflecting
the bright hearths of the lost.

Mystic

I have seen God   O Yes.
Don't fondle me with doubt
or any lowercase vanity,
or drugs, those footnotes
to excess.
I have ascended a moment
dry as Assisi
and seen the sky turn inside out.

The reflection of cities shimmered
in the same violence,
men continued to wear
their faces like shields,
money answered the same wounds,
everything
tasted the same.

But the roots of the dead cried out
We are your children.
We grow.
Listen.
And the alphabet flew into the sun,
taking our names with it,

leaving us
everywhere with these losses,
this incomparable
nothing:

it settles on my shoulder
like a bird.

Nomads

Mirages

Well, I have given
them to anyone who asked.

No one ever came back.

Perhaps they were real.

A Good End

When death rises in the east,
exhausting the desert with light,

I will empty my glassful of deceptions
into the sand:

that flowing
will sing more lucidly
than the emperor's nightingale

who knew
to what dry brilliance
all mirages converge.

The Barker

The only thing non-
repetitious on the midway is
the barker. He believes
in the rarities he calls
his listeners to, believes
so far beyond questions
in what he hasn't seen
that his voice, his own
voice, is itself
a conviction.
           I see
thousands enter that show
expecting what they see
to correspond with,
to be,
what they have heard.
           I see
them, all,
return, incredulous, dis-
appointed, return
to accept again
these preferable sentences
from a novelty
man
whose terms change.

The Midget

About growing up
the midget did
not think
to take his time.
It was everything
at once or
nothing at all. He
tried, regardless: appears
at present one,
exponent n, a power
divisible by
himself,
capable, now
that he puts
his mind to it,
only of redundancy.

Chief of freaks,
he gets away
like a professional
with anything, looks
harmless, gives
advice; sometimes
imagines himself
part of a royal
personage but separated
from the whole by
time. Regrets
aloud his age.

One
thing he has yet

to learn: to be
content with:
the size
of truth.

The Ballad of the Three Birds

Left to himself and his invitations
The man of parts declined,
And nothing in the declining world
Could change his mind.

The way was short, the way was long,
The beginning bore the end,
And sufficient unto any day
Was that day's dividend.

He walked the sufficient evening
Surmounted by his hat;
He met himself returning
And that was that.

A bird perched above the body
Confirmed his eminence:
He troubles the way of angels,
He knows what he wants.

Wanted, said the second bird
Who had decorum of his own.
For my part there's nothing sweeter
Than an upright man.

Flesh is flesh, the third bird said
Whether upright or not:
Whatever moves under God's eye
Moves by appetite.

The first bird ate his eyes and tongue,
The second cleaned his thighs,

The third bird picked his testicles,
Which were small and dry.

His bones pall unencumbered,
The birds wait on the wind;
What is well served beneath God's eye
Meets in their mind.

THE HERMAPHRODITE

That miracle
of science the Half
Man Half Woman,
divided into a Garden
of Eden where only the one
who offers the apple
eats it,
squints each eye
against the withering
glare of
the midway, seems
to level
everything
in sight, delivering
the unspoken
message *We
know you.*

THE BALLAD OF THE SCARECROW

Those in whose image I am made
Must thrive on enmity;
How else can it be understood
That birds are afraid of me?

I would have them crest my shoulders
And flutter at my feet;
I mark the wind's vague winnowings
And bear no fruit.

I wait, if this is waiting,
I cast a minor shade;
They catch a flick of sleeve and go
Unsettled and denied.

I have watched the finch design his air,
The flicker rise, and lighten;
Why is the bright seed sown or strewn
If not to be eaten?

I have watched them shape their distances
Weaving every weather,
Rendering what I stand up for
Not worth a feather.

Those in whose image I am made
Should hold their ground more lightly.
I cast my storied lendings off
And watch them blow away.

Songs for Champagne Saturday

(1978)

Songs for Champagne Saturday

1

My remarkable body has
all its life

transformed grain into blood,
and three times
blood into replicas of itself,

but nothing in 40 years
prepared it

to live without you.

2

If I were to say how
I miss you
you would know
how laughter

can be as the departure of birds
from winter, their songs from winter.

3

The sun rains.
I drink the entire desert
of my life, and I am
still thirsty.

This is what I bring you.

4

Do other lives
also swing
between grief and longing,

for which the limp
and the stiff prick
are the simplest signs?

I remember my father
winter mornings
                            beginning
to tie his shoes
in the dark.

5
I spent 20 years
writing a book wholly from grief,
burning with loss.

Now

you are more lovely to me
than the whole fire.

6
I keep time with you
in the long absences. A wall
of years opens silently as a flower
and I enter you through it.

If my children
could be the children of another
they would be yours, they would call me
the name you teach them,

and I would rise from my drawn cells
and become their father.

from
COMMON GROUND
(1982)

TURNTABLES
for Darren

A grooved disc, a sliver of diamond, and the music rises;

His darkened eyes, the ribbon of birth
Cut: and the influential squawl
Thrilling the air—
                within which breath is drawn,
Within which the race is to the quickest,
Within which the race stories itself—
                      rises;

Above me today the dry air reflecting
The dry grass, a shimmer of heat between,
Inescapable. *Stand in this* the season says.
Neither air nor time grows into anything else
Though they circle forever, our lives lifting music.
Stand it says *where you are:*
                  in a small room
His small body, new in the air,
                    filling it;

The human music. The awful human music.

That'll Be the Day

for Quentin Vest

I

Sweet Anna Gram is not
The lightsome plaything you like to think
She is. I go beyond
Zed and zygote, and there she is prancing,
Showing off, moving from one volute to another,
Denying nobody the smallest liberty, the smallest
Adjustment of illusion.
                    For years
I thought she played to a packed house,
But I mistook the brilliance of the spotlights
Focused on her for the audience: I forgot
Use is not performance, and she is nothing
If not used.
                    Nonetheless,
In all the parodies of vengeance the rest of us
Enact, no one approaches
The exquisite balance of her attention:

We say *live,* and she gives us *lie*
And *evil,* or
Is evil itself false? or
The whole composite
Vile? In *death* she hides our appetite,
In *love* a stringy rodent
Who can take all the tricks in the game.
                              These are
The big words, I'm trying to be honest:
                              live
Eat, love, die, are the permanent injunctions;

It's hard to imagine
She dances with them at random.

2

As long as it's someone else
Who's loving her, or saying so,
I can manage, but when I try to speak
To her, I have to cordon off the voices:
They don't quite echo each other.
They don't seek her the same way,
Or seek the same her, or seek anything
Beyond their own seeking sound.

They aren't
Conscious of me. They stay on their side
Of the ropes, but I feel them threatening.
Haven't I sent you after her? Haven't I
Released you forever? I ask, multiplying
Them, dividing myself among them.

Is this
Like life, I wonder, the lie
Cloistered in *belief,* the rut in *truth,* the truth
In everything, and like this, the praise
In *despair,* the am in *game* and *grammar,*
The increasing scar,

the tenure of return, the father
Disguising hate, what can I do with the rat
In generation?

No tentative man
In his right mind could create such a mob
And expect to survive it in one piece.

3

Anna,
This is goodbye. I'm calling
It quits. I'm going to be
Someone else. I don't care
If it is the same alphabet, I can learn
To make all my voices

Forget you. It doesn't matter
How the lines string out, how many syllables fondle
Each other in the dark
Wishing I were back, how often you don't exist
Because I don't talk you into it. It's not
My problem anymore. I plan
To become lovable, and move
Into the real world where nobody listens.

BEGGING ON NORTH MAIN

Should I worry about choosing
The right word if I can get what I want
By pointing at it?
             What do I want?
                     Is it this ghost
With the unslakable past, this rusty child
Who keeps asking me to give him his eyes back?

Is it the stone man who disappears
Beneath my toes every step I take,
Telling me he's nobody's thoroughfare?
                    If I were dreaming
Would I call them both *Father*
And follow them blind into the center of the earth?
Would I come out bright-eyed and raw on the other side
In a country whose people speak in pictures,
Where someone could say *Look*, and point,
And I would see my self?

It's hard to ask the right questions,
                    yet the fire I have
Kindled with my vocabulary and its hungry years
Gives off a growing heat,
              and the day I saw
My reflection in its bottom I gave my tin cup
To the mute on North Main Street.
When he sees me coming he smiles
And points the cup at me, slowly turning it
Until it flashes the sun into my face.

KILLDEER
for Nathan

One, and then another, they settled before me
        like flakes of air,
Halfway up the hill, their splayed toes sketching
Shadows, the grass tufts, gravel, merging;
They came down from their marvelous fluency
To wobble on dumb stilts
Like earthbound creatures, hindered by strangeness.
The shadows were blue and voluminous, and their toes lost,
And the pronouns confused, and they shied and took flight
Again as I drove the rest of the way up the hill.
When I entered the house
And called my wife to the window they were back,

                                                        settled,
Settled into the dark; and in the Blue Ridge morning
They parted, again, for my descent.
                                They were there
Every day the last seven months before the gift,
Feathering my passage
Like wings, their angled wings, her shoulder blades
As she bent awkwardly before the sink, mornings,
In the ninth month.

So that my father, who we thought was dying,
Could see him, we carried his newborn grandson
Up the back stairs of the hospital. The light was broken
All over the blanket, and our child swam in his glasses
With pieces of that broken light.
                                Their russet throats,
The sun shattered in the gravel,
                                the gray veins
Of his impeccable wrist,
                        Lord, for the life of me.

When we brought him home they had flown away.

Elegies for Walker Dabney Stuart, Jr. (1901–1971)

Dark So Early, Dark So Long

The dead injure me with attentions, and nothing can happen.

It's always too early,
No one is ever *quite* ready, but neither
Is a man to be measured by his intentions, the lordly avenues
He dreams of, the chimes, the fileted hour.
When the time comes, it comes.
     The front
If the mirror reflects my face, an expectation;
But if I turn the mirror over in my hand, its back
Reveals the back of my head. That's where I am,
In a center between expectation and surprise,
Where nothing happens.
     My dead, your waking
Rocks me, waking.
    What life was it
He was so devoted to? Every day his attendance was perfect,
But the files spill, the papers scatter;
Do his eyes stay closed in the locked dirt,
The meticulous box?
     Do not
   Mistake me. I have come
   Here because I want

   To come here. What I have
   Lost compels me to

   Come here. Someone
   Has spirited away, all

   Right, much. More.
   It burns. Heat rises. Jack,

Be nimble, Jack,
Be quick, Jack,

Don't you know once dead there's no more dying?
Pull yourself together, here's Walker now, it's 1920,

                                                    he comes to play.

Though the Red and Blue schedules him as a breather
He comes to *shock 18,000 fans by ripping*
The Red and Blue to pieces, playing the best game
At quarter seen on Franklin Field this Fall;

                                   he's suited up,

He moves through the broken field like a butterfly,
Does a Jubal Early down the sideline
With a stolen pass, soaring—

                          such heights,

Such luminous edges—

                   no Penn team
Was ever outclassed more or beaten worse
Than the Red and Blue eleven yesterday.

                        Yesterday.

The very word,
            death's feather in my cap.

                           And when the game

Ended, the seasons
Ended, the last reunion hale and golden ended, he comes home,
           to my home,
Crosses the threshold, gives up what poise
Had let him dance that string of pearls,
Not once, but Lord these fifty years,

And I undress and dress and lay him down.

No more. My sorrow is not dead.

       Do not mistake me.
I have come here because there is no other place.
It may be that death is peace, that the tiger

Lies down with the lamb, that the jackal
Speaks dulcetly with the mourning dove, that all
Will be well, and all manner of thing will be well,

But my tongue is dry, the nice quietude
Hemmed with thorns, and everything
Unseasonable, warped, unstrung.
                              When it's done
It is not done. I want to be quick, spirited myself,
To call toward the dread air irrational embodiments
Like
        Hey Fulsome! Hey Guts!
You see this brand-new, secondhand flyswatter?
It's for you, and I'm a deadeye with it; stay back,
You can prey, yes indeedy, prey, but not on carrion,
No, on a source,
A light, a cluster of vitality, radiant, wheeling you,
And I'm right here in the middle singing shoo-fly,
Go away from my doors, my thresholds,
The places where we cross,

The bodies of my death my life.

It is not done until I say it's done.

The Life You Live May Be Your Own
Who knowes not Arlo-hill?

                I

He has been undivided for a month:
He does not breathe.
His body does not tremble with the desire to breathe.
He is not seized, nothing seizes him;
He no longer angers himself by his dependence
On those who mistake their refusal to pity him
For love.

An unobtrusive man who is responsible
For the success of others may compensate
For the praise he does not get publicly
By praising himself in private. Sometimes
He grows louder, more often. The focus of his stories
Closes toward a center. He seems repetitive, mere
Hot air. This is a form of desperation, a longing
For those measureless instants
When there was no audience,
An ineffectual rebuttal of time, as all our speaking is,
And no less worthy because it is common.

Remembering is not so much a desire to live something
Over again, as it is regret for having lived
At all.

The face of all earthly things is changed.

2

                                                  Old friend,
Swollen air, how we gone get *to* this gone
Old friend? His troubles are over no doubt
About that, he wheezed to the end
Of them, not least, nor the tossed rises, bone
Of his last dog's bed. I reckon he got out
And in about ten times a night, then he got out
Past time. Lord.
                     We got to deflate pard-
ner, learn how to say it straight one of these days,
Can't let it rest, bad doings, our first onliest stay
Against the world's most regiment done
Joined up. He wanted, finally, that. Say when.

3
It begins. It had begun
Before these words joined in their long distress,

86

Settling toward rhythm and its darker eye
As a stone through sinking water.

Even from down here I believe one day
My life will be full of a lot more
Than your death and its mordant dross,

Yet death is the talker's goad, or we'd be still
And our wayward voices creating everything
Would thin forever on the unsteady air,
No different from breath, which even dumb creatures draw.

Even as I seem to see
A school of angel fish it veers, dissolves, becomes
Mere coral, or sky-blue creatures of another eye
Than mine. My stillness centers
Nothing; it is impossible to follow
Such diversity of motion anywhere. I don't need
To go deeper than a foot to be lost, to be turned
Back into a creature of questions, prying
Shoreward, wondering

Would I live on snails and mussels?
Would I choose to starve? If I were about to be eaten
Would I defend myself so well
No one would recognize me anymore?
Would I try to become invisible? Is that the only way
To anticipate attack from any angle?
                                        When
My son's foot was pierced by the spines of a sea urchin
The beach people told me I had my choice
Of going down on my knees before him and pissing on his wounds
Or binding him up and seeking out the amputator.
It wasn't prayer, but it worked.
For a week men glistening from the sea, muscled, lyrical,
Would stop and stare at his instep,
As if its pattern of black mottle were a fading sign,
A talisman, beyond questions, beyond belief.
                                        Who
Could ask for anything more?
                        These creatures don't.
They continue to swim,
To eat.
They move away from me, they move

Away.
     If peace exists anywhere it exists here, under
Water—
         my ears fill with it, it leaks into my mask—
                       where
What little that is asked is answered,
Always, under
Water,
     which I would raise
Like a goblet—this small bay containing everything
More or less—to you, brave child who refused to cry,
Whose pain my urine eased, who learns to swim
Behind a mask like mine.

An Interlude at the Grand Hotel

This is no mail-order bride, nor a lyrical impulse
To be tricked out in beads and blossoms for a soupçon
Of matrimony *al fresco*. Nor a one-night stand.
Alone,
She looks across the lake toward something
Out of focus. Or at the air. If she removed
The broad-brimmed, filigreed hat, her brown hair
Would cascade all the way to her hips. Her lace cuffs
And the embroidered hem of her skirt
Edge the delicate bosses
Of her wrists and ankles, and her drawn waist
Moves slightly as she breathes. She is
Altogether composed.
                        The silhouette
Of privacy does not wish to entice,
As certain markings of butterflies have nothing
To do with the business of survival.
                                    The intricate
Crazings on this hotel porcelain
Weren't decorative, but a map of sensibility;
And these columns:
When she came here in the old days
She saw, without trying, the web of hairthin lines
In the marble, and called that marble. An eye for
The tenuous, the fine pattern of fragility
Along whose lines everything breaks, becoming
Visibly the pieces of itself it always was:
A crystalline vision,
                        the source of style.
                                    I imagine
Her turning
Her head from the flat lake water and beginning to look

Down the long line of shore. The sunlight catches
A few wisps of hair, bronzing them, but
Her visible eye remains in shadow.
                                    She has
Breakfast in bed, the complacency of high ceilings;
A lover
Or not doesn't matter, the touch of flesh and sheet
Is sexual, cellular with longing.
                              The pores
Invite.
      The breeze through the pines contends.
                                          Her window
Has eighteen panes,
                  nor is the surface of the lake
                                          glass.
The world promises nothing, because it is.

No Yellow Jackets on the Mountain
for Mike Martin

Friendship turns. And turns again. Another name
For history, the mimes of history

                        end-

less

    exercises, webs of language
Preceding us, spun brotherhoods into which we fall
As we are born, learning to speak to each other.

Ten years ago you stopped chasing
The cities of the Western world as if they were women,
Abandoned the mazes of *strasses* and *allées*
And freight yards, and came back to Virginia
To build a cabin on Big Walker Mountain.
Since then I've climbed it a half dozen times
To speak with you, passing
The trail's forks and the forked trees, one tree
Writhing upward past its fractured limb, above
The bloodroot and wintergreen, until
I can dream it so clearly the whole ascent
Seems part of the talk itself, composed—
Except for the light beyond the unsettled leaves
Casting these flickered shadows—as a poem
Is composed.
              And yet
The light in a poem
Is like no other light, nor like itself,
Shining as it does through a network
Which is also its source.
                       Can poetry
Glow in the dark, then? With darkness?
Can a friend? What kind of luminous mesh

Is strong enough to sustain the complexities
Of friendship? What is sufficient?
                                        Your life
Seems to crumble
Like rotted wood to the touch.
One day the wind will rise
And disperse it over the mountain:
Have you wished for this from the beginning?
                                        I remember
Your hand burrowing in a chestnut stump,
Fingering the cool loam, then suddenly withdrawn,
Already swelling with the hidden sting.
                                        And today
I climb the mountain again, leaning
Against its pitch, listing
Past broken
Causes, twisted
Growth, wanting again
To give it up, turn back, missing
The highwire joy that keeps a man
Working at these heights from letting go.

I rest on a rock. I find myself

Staring down at the valley, my eyes
Filled with the railroad tracks' dazzling
Twin silver, playing their usual trick
Of joining beyond sight, denying themselves.

Meanwhile, the blue shadows on the leaving trees,
The early petals, fallen, the predictable transactions,
Departures, a mountain cabin—
Paper littering a table, a heated stone—
These are never sufficient, but they remain
Clues to places, or a place:
They too reflect a light.

Does love end here? Or a man's work?
Here? Among this endless language?
                                        Clearly
From where I sit
The last word is a myth, and neither
Love nor work, that crossed
Conundrum, answers it.
                        As clearly,
Space divides according to a basic need
For—what? Privacy? To be privy
Only to one's necessities? To find
Among these partial stations time, anonymous
Concentration, for the simple move
That will make one rich, or to cry

Mommy in the dark as one possessed
Might seek to call forth from himself
His favorite mirror? It has resolved
Nothing; to judge from the writing on the walls
Neither has a siege of palpation and nibblement
Tidbitwise on the ticking. Nope.
                                Nevertheless, this is
A viable location, a verbal environment of some
Friendliness, a variable surround. Adjacent
To the tissue holder (empty in my stall)
The famous Big Bucks with Short Horns imperative
Reasserts itself; on the door so I may read it
From a commodious position is the modest maxim
Concerning the distance between literature
And the bowl (so to speak); elsewhere
Heartbreak and characterization occur,

Appointments are suggested, complete
With numbers for those inexperienced
In certain areas, and of course
There are the usual cave drawings depicting
Tribal customs and the dream life of the master race.
All the impressions are sizable, clearly
This is a place for people who care,
An imaginable community with a past, a forum—

                                    as I stood

In fact, a shimmer of the air across the room
Appeared to coalesce into both wall and words,
A tablet, which I read aloud:

> When I began to love and fight
> I kept my language out of sight;
> Now that I own most of the world
> I prattle like a mindless girl.
> Does it always come to this, O Zeus,
> The upright staff, the torrid juice,
> Empire and *amor* politics
> Reduced to bathhouse limericks:
> It's too much for this verbose geezer
> Who signs *his* graffiti, Julius Caesar.

Ambitious, yes—more polished at least
Than the later scratchings I had previously
Encountered, but still
Local,
        tempered by the writer's immediate
Perplexity,
And neither weightier nor more historical than
Want some? Try Phyllis 771-1101.
                        I felt relieved. I
Zipped up, smoothed out, and shoved off,
                              elated

With the concert
Of human
Being
        and my part in it, all the way
In, I figure, doing what I can
To spread the word.

Finding One of the Ghosts

Love hid everywhere, including
The sour corners of his own memory;
He called to it, his voice reedy with longing,
But when he tried to confront it directly
He found nothing but salt talking.

Would I lure a rabbit with pork? he wondered.
Much less, then, love with promises.
He had given her more than he could promise
As it was, and what had it gotten him?

One mute servitude after another, bowing
Toward each vacuum she set before him
Until he hunched under the bottom shelf
Of the deepest closet, believing
Any brief crack in the door was morning.
                                        It looked

Hopeless. *I might as well imagine*
The motion of a wing without a wing,
Or try to float a stone he said

And opened the door, wide, the simplest gesture.

After all
These years he had arrived at her level, and could look
Her in the eye.

            It has taken me a while

To raise myself again through that surprise
But I am standing up now;
My eyes have adjusted to the light: I begin

To see a fading version of myself,
A suitcase in each hand, shuffling
Out the door, Old Baggy Pants, not quite
Chaplin, not quite my father. I wave
But he doesn't turn around,
Just keeps leaving. One day he'll be gone.

COMMON GROUND

It was a cool season, full of reserve
When the animals drew back
Into their memories, as if
They were hoarding something, saving it up
For the right time. There are no calendars
For such withdrawal, but perhaps
One of them saw its shadow
And ducked back down its hole, leaving the air
Shapeless with absence.
                        If you believe
Today is always an exception
                        you will never be a hero.

In an episode of The Wild Wild Old Days with Clever Gadgets
The heroine warns the hero, urgently, limpidly,
Not to go back in time with the villain whose mind   -
Controls matter, because he might never come back to the present,
And the hero says, urgently, distantly, *If there is a 4th*
Dimension—and I believe there is—then I must
Find out if it is a threat
To the security of my country.

Everybody had trouble sleeping, the children
Were feverish for no apparent reason, birthday parties
Were canceled, pets of all kinds
Were still and silent,
                        there was a cortege of weather.

On another channel the captain of the spaceship
Told an alien life-form who spoke his language
But whom he couldn't see (pure energy or something)
There's not room enough in this galaxy for both of us.

Dis make de udder Crawfishes mighty mad,
en dey sorter swarmed togedder en draw'd up
a kinder peramble wid some wharfo'es in it,
en read her out in de 'sembly. But, bless grashus!
sech a racket was a gwine on dat nobody ain't hear it,
'ceppin maybe de Mud Turkle en de Spring Lizzud,
en dere enfloons was pow'ful lackin'.
                                    So dar dey wuz,
de Crawfishes, en dey didn't know w'at minnit
wuz gwinter be de nex'; en dey kep' on gittin madder
en madder en skeerder en skeerder, twel bimeby
dey gun de wink ter de Mud Turkle en de Spring Lizzud,
en den dey bo'd little holes in de groun' en went down

outer sight.

            If the earth were someday
Filled with the pressure of such shrewd joy,
                                    what
Fountains there would be, what
Flowing. The ladies would sashay and the children
Gambol, old words bloom. Even now it wells up:

This child of mine lies on his side on the floor,
One leg drawn up under the other,
His head resting on a forearm,
Listening.

from
DON'T LOOK BACK
(1987)

THE BIRDS
for Nathan

1

                    That midwinter day
you could almost
say the sandpipers ambled, hungry,
their bright eyes cocked
toward the minute pores glinting
in the sand—
              ambled
almost,
        but when the next wave broke
and spread toward them
they broke, too, sprinting
back up the beach, break-
neck, their brittle legs flailing
like pendulums gone mad.

They always outran the sea,
but they seemed barely to touch it, too,
to keep no distance; it was as if
they drew each wave in after them,
not fleeing at all, and then followed it
back as it withdrew: one motion,
bird and water, water
and bird, serene,
a paradigm.

2

                    Sometimes in the dead
middle of the night when the knot
under my sternum tightens and presses upward
as though it would part my rib cage
and hatch itself,

I place the forefinger of one hand
on the thin vein winging my other wrist
and feel beat there my father's
puzzled belief that a life is always edging
toward itself, that if enough be done,
be gotten through, today, then tomorrow a man's
dream of himself might settle down
out of the distant air onto his shoulder,
flutter its wings a little, and at last
rest,

that such success would take the place of death,
of history, of time.
                          I touch my wrist: his
life
goes on, it goes
on; I am unsettled, too,
by this conviction, that one day
my imagination will draw all
that it releases
back into itself.

      3
Sandpiper, killdeer, mourning dove, quail,
how can you fly with a salted tail?

Ask the old crow on the split rail

Rock bird, water bird, bird of woe,
what do you eat in the spring snow?

Ask the crow

When your craw is empty, how do you sing?
Can you make shift with a cracked wing?

The crow knows everything

When you can't manage a stiff wind
what shelter do you find?

The crow's kind

Dry bird, broken bird, bird of gray,
how do you get through a bad day?

The crow's way

Birds of my life,
birds of my air, my song's mouth,
what are your answers worth?
Give me the practical truth.

You don't fool us with your litany
You don't wonder what, how, why
You want to know how to die

Look in the crow's eye.

4

One-a-penny, two-a-penny, they settled
like flakes of air:

ducks on a pond.

When Remington-Peters set my father in the blind
once a year in the prime of the season
he never hit anything.
He never hit anything
when they set him in the field, either,
with the best dogs pointing,
the startled quail whirring
upward from the hedges.

                                   When he
             aimed from the blind, or raised
             his dull gun in the dull day
             to the flushed covey,
                                   the birds flew
             on the blank surface of his glasses,

             free there,

             like he is, here.

                   5
             It's ten o'clock in April again. It's snowing.
             Nine years ago today two killdeer courted
             my first son into the world: their incredible wings

             will bend within his wrists as long as he lives. Blood
             brothers. We are in Athens, Ohio;
             everyone's cellar is filling with water, maybe

             in celebration of my father's grandson's turning
             into his tenth year in the mixed seasons
             filling the city with spring snow, spring flood;

             it seems such pressure could unmoor it
             and send it floating over the Appalachians seaward
             into West Virginia; the light would fly up

             out of the pine trees, startled, flocking.
             If it veered northward
             we might understand

             that all along it has been a migration like this
             the mourning doves wonder about out loud.
             Even now they call toward the lost light.

In such a time, in April, you could almost imagine
a child standing under the pines,
shadowed. He could lift his hand to them

and open it, releasing among their needles
an affable light, a flying instant
which might nest in them, a birthday covenant

of the impossible flight.

THE GIRL OF MY DREAMS

How she would welcome my hands
into her body. The beat of her heart
depended on the skill of my massage!
Evenings after work
she would put on her best breasts
and sweater, float into my head
for a good feel. She would say
I like your eyes on me—even now
I sometimes mistake them for hers.
Her voice was always a combination
of my own and my mother's.
Such mutual devotion. By looking
through me she could create herself,
and I could take her with me unscathed
into the future, where
she would invariably choose me
over all comers. *There's no one else*
but me we would promise each other,
writing our names with chalk on the sidewalk.
When I played catch she would be thousands
cheering in the bleachers. Even now
I hear her calling *I am everywhere*
you put yourself. Take me.

CASTING

1

Once upon a time does well enough
to begin with, because the time went slow
then, an air we moved in,
a place to settle, like stones downward
in dark water, bottomless.
And how we drifted
    —into each other's
slow motion your brilliant hair awash,
disheveled on me; what distances
we brought together, all future there
in that loose light untangling, all
that waking
    —into sons,
gifts of the first water, whose making
bore the simple
astonishment of parting
and again parting, the blind coming
becoming, not once but twice
    —into this life,
a wholly imaginary vision

but the real thing, as all lives are wherein
no one lives happily ever after.

2

If it seems nothing much happened, it is
because we made no language for what happened,
made our experience everyone's experience,
believing without doubt or consciousness
we were immortal, which is to say

the whale of what we were and were doing
in the world swallowed us up.

    3
Slow time
in that dark, slow motion, *I*
love I said *you,*
and you conceived sons.
                       I cut
a hole in the ice, sent my line down,
said *I love* of all people *you,*
and you skated circles around me.
                          In the eye
of that tousled light I said nothing,
my empty mouth open, full of the sources
of speech, and you brought forth sons.
                           I looked
at them, delicate, saw their names would be
distance, and said through it
I love and *you,*
                feeling in some blind depth
a stirring, which I struck gently,
gingerly, with furious restraint, and

hooked.

And let run, easing the drag. And run.

It runs still, no matter what
I bring to your table.

I remember that morning
when mornings were years, you came down
to the coffee and bacon whose smells
had wakened you, and I pointed

to three bass, gutted, on the drainboard.
I opened the mouth of one
wide enough to take in all Virginia,
and we opened ours.

Later to the sweetness still on my tongue,
to the feel of the taut line humming still
in my fingers, to you
still on my tongue, replete in the long morning,
I said

I love.

4
What can I say
to you now, Motherwife,
when ten years seem a day?
Can words, or words' echo,
release from this gathered life
an image of its needs,
as quick motion, or its shadow,
scatters the school from the reeds?

If they can, and if you could
see it and respond, how
would I know?
Though I still
sit at center ice
is that really you at play
on the far edges, teasing
my taut will?

If, in the devious
and poised tricks
of our sometime sex—

that slippery rage—
I can't make a match
fit for the mute turbulence
of this middle age,
must I go find some witch

who will teach me to brew
my life from old books,
and conjure, and construe,
and raise, if not the dead,
lost selves instead
to love, and grapple with
in the dustbed of myth:
i.e., turn to nothing worse

than the pitched depth of verse?
Nobody comes. Nobody
answers. I would say nothing's
left but to go down,
take a slow dive
to the poor dim bottom
where the mirrors live
were it not pure tedium
there, without solace,

and crowded to boot. Malice,
like the many-humped serpent
of old maps, keeps watch
from his corner. I nod,
turn my back, decide
to hang on, play the fine catch
on this silly instrument
again. Silence, please.

This is my last reprise.

5

If it's a dream
only a person from the dream
can wake me.
                    No
one is there.
                    I
hold the monofilament
at the lure's eye
suspended. A light
breaks upon it
a fine shower of gold.

Dazzled
        I
bend closer, my hand
misguiding, missing

such a simple act,
threading
the bait's eye.
                    I
continue to
fail
        seemingly forever
bowed
toward the shimmering brightness

blurred—so close,
now so many times

my mouth is
littered with hooks.

Once More for My Lady

1

No matter how gently, with what suspended
fierceness, from however deep a well
of passion longing to be lifted, oblivious,

                                  no
matter how gently you touch a woman,
if she does not wish to be touched
or, wishing, does not wish yours, does not begin
to turn away
from the grottoed vista of her self

                                 toward
the future hovering between
your barely perceptible hand and her flesh,

then it is no different from brute ice
laid on with a mason's trowel.

2

                              How often,
most loved woman, did you turn
your husband into a bricklayer?

                            Did he become
just another man who gave occasion
for your fondest ceremonies—the least
of which got you children—and then receded?
Those raucous energies I remember
echoing from the grease pit of his boat—
was it you who compressed them finally
into his tinkling glass, and the raw curse
of his last, contagious years?

                            When you saw him
stricken, desolate, supine, mindless,
his days dribbling through the slack lips,

did the image come unbidden
of him young again, at no one's mercy
then but yours? Did he
lead you far enough out of your self once,
or enough, to make you remember now,
honoring him unknowing with that palimpsest
grief no grave posture satisfies?
Did you reach out to the image?

3

Your laced aloofness straitened your husband.

To me, who didn't know the stakes yet, it seemed
exemplary, the only way things were.

Before I could
imagine sex, conceive
a trite fold, or probe
or mazy wander
in any lady's chamber,
                    you set out
these determinations in the room I slept in:

a crazed
porcelain ewer, off-white, a matching
basin, and, under the bed, a chamber pot
with its cold lip, a cut-
glass decanter webbed
with starbursts of spirits, the ghosts
of spirits, crystal snowcrystal,
crystallized camphor—
                    even now you present to me
in dreams
pitcher, bowl, pot, decanter
set on a plateau of veined marble
you bear before you, raised,
a salver.

You bow.

Your white hair descends about you, robing.

4

Heartbeat, what else could you be?
An interlude at the grand hotel,
throb for a passing drummer, high-C
at a woman's club solo, slow belle
of the ball in a pressed book
of scraps and tag ends? No, of
course not, not when the first look
to the last spasm and crack of love
was one long portrait to be tested
against the future: a full career,
a conception. You never rested
from it until, near eighty, your
own death started to craze
the canvas, mute its colors, score
those old configurations, amaze
the horizon, me, everyone—you.
You weren't immune. How simple. Life,
and the art it conjured up, became
the last thing you'd expect, an empty frame.
Too neat, too simple? No. For you,
though more than mother, widow, wife,
and type of these, lived to discover
you were also fiercely less.
Before it was over
you had nothing left to bless

and blessed it.

5

These are the desolate, sad days,
when the crow sits on the fencepost
cawing his gross syllable

and we stuff our dumb fingers
into the wounds of the planet
to prove it palpable, present, real.

The air in this paneled den thickens
with memory and dust:
where I sit, the shaft of sunlight

prods my shins and the low table,
the base of the crazed spinet;
I hear the crow's flight diminish

his long-winded spiel.
To increase distance, the poet says,
is to decrease pain. Maybe. But the singers

of darkness know the past quickens
when you wait on it, attending,
and know the dead never finish

asking their questions of your life.
I open the window.

                Your life
        is over, Grandmother: it was

        almost as ordered as these stanzas
        are, more obvious and severe
        in its gentility. But the ending

        didn't fit, that cancerous claw
        dragging and digging at your teeth
        until it tore away the whole jaw.

        The doctors could stuff that with gauze,
        drug it dumb, but the raw ghost
        that burned in the char of your eyes

responded to nothing but death.
Through those last long weeks
I kept seeing

the trenchant jaw and austere cheekbone
of your marvelous face,
an immortal profile, cause

and brunt of love, the priming face—
kept seeing burn in your fierce eyes
far off that desperate ghost, as though

I looked through binoculars
the wrong way. In another age
that would be an image

for the depths of your soul. All I know
is that you stared through me, neither slept
nor spoke, and then died, your scars

intact.

        This room, this window, this light
scar me now. A long life wants crust.
Those last mute weeks peeled hers to the quick

and she willed me the vision. We give
what we can, all right, and I live
with this, finding it neither trick

nor secret, finding not truth
inscrutable, but the ways
we manage it. She left me dust

and a wrack of light to float
it in, a trapped shadow in the shape
of a bird to roost on it and bring

forth from its exorbitant throat
the sound of grief
in the form of celebration.

Taking the Wheel

I

It's you and me again, Duststroke,
Curseworld. Until you spoke
to me in the midst of my own words
it had seemed a peaceful decade
between us. Now the old wind swells;
its movement in my throat, on my forehead,
reminds me we have been standing in it
together all this time without reprieve:
silence is no less a place than any other.

I know what your life came to,
how it ended: the splitbrain wrack
addling on the pillow beside your mouth,
the damned lock growing in your jaw.
God damn it to hell you kept shouting,
repeating your last words for three years
infinitely, as if speech itself
is a rock we break
against, or a passage with frozen gates
we enter, and enter, until we are stoven in.
Welcome you tell me now, your voice as clear
in my head as a buoy's bell in raw fog.

I could sail halfway around the world
in a closed cabin with the shades drawn, and learn
as much as you ever taught me about death.
It's taken me this long to see that as your gift.
You made me heir to the intricate fierce spaces
which lead only to each other, and are called life;
and the curse you laid like a rope in my hand
leads over the side again, disappears

in the dark reaches where it's all one,
where it begins.
                    The first time I tried
to be fish—
finning wide-eyed through the drowning water,
happy to change my nature—
I never wanted to come back, give up that warm
release from everything, being all over.
But you pulled me out anyway, set me adrift
on the ground again, kicking and crying,
as if to say *Shove off, it's not that easy.*

Now it appears I have to answer
the rope's pull again, follow it under
the maps, make up my mind, stand at the wheel
of this dustraft and dive.
                    I can
hear my sons
in the next room munching their sleep.
One of them turns, pulling his blanket
up over his backside; tomorrow is stacked
on their dressers, waiting to be put on.
Saving me for myself is a long pull
with no guarantee, Grandfather, but together
I might find out what it means to accept and grieve.

        2

My first son was born
twelve years on the wrong side
of your death. I am torn
to write this twenty-one
years in the same direction.

When I was nine
I rode a black horse free
on your small-time

beach carousel;
that fake calliope

music seemed to make
its circle go round,
my horse slide up
and down
on its golden pole: double mime
of this life.
          Once, my stirrup
snapped while I stood
waving my hat to the crowd;
as I fell everything
tilted, the mad
music swarmed
over me, was nothing
to hold on to, my head
jarred on the bright wood.

The Rollercoaster you owned—
snaking its trite arcs—
and the sudden
Tunnel of Love diving
into the waves
of light, also took
me their tracked ways;
I have been thrown down
by their like, too.

My sons can be sure
to get all that and more
before they're through.

But they missed you.

3

The farthest reach
of my dark mind through darkness
is nothing to your sweet

grapple, the pull of your arms
through the long, viscid years.
You were the first

man in the world to know
how to make me welcome, to see
the wheel of light binding my head

and body in an early photograph
as me, a focus. Is that why
you hauled me out of the drowning water,

or is saving life
a reflex, like cursing?
Whatever it was that made you

bring me up,
I hear now beneath my words
your voice in my mind say *Welcome.*

You will die as I died,
paralyzed, speech
stuck in your jaw like a cud

and know it to be fear
standing at the wheel and diving
at the same time, drowning in air.

Don't Look Back

1

I walk through the high-ceilinged
yesterday of forever. Nobody's
in there who's supposed to be.
I want the legend
of bubbling glasses and happy people
in all the rooms, family
like I dreamed of when the real people
were there with their fake cheer.
I want them to be mine,
their warmth to lift me into the domes
with the other angels.
I laugh, and it's still
all gone, an empty never.

2

In one party room the yesterday
people clutter, I
stumble on a rug. *Don't
just lie there* an uncle says
and sits on my chest.
Get something up. Everyone
lifts their glasses and pours
ice cubes on my groin:
To your future sons they call out.
*May they rise and rise
until you are just a man
lying on a rug in an empty
gone.* Like I am.
It would be enough if someone,
any ghost, would come
and sit in the window.

He could say something, or not,
just being,
and I could breathe deeply
and let it all out.

3

Or in the kitchen where the black women
wear gardenias
in their hair
and hum to the kettle.
The steam makes little beads
of water quiver
on the ceiling. And such food!
Even the desperate people
who live in their 100-proof
glasses grow tame eating it.
It's all gone, I lie
on the rug under the table
listening for the lost voices
of the black women
murmuring as they clear.

The Girl of My Dreams Is Dying

I bend over her but she waves
me off. *I don't need you*
anymore she says. *This is no time*
to fool around I tell her.
This is death. I try to take
her hand, all I want
is to comfort her, but she jerks
it away. She tries to cup
her breasts and thrust them
toward me but her fists
knot the blanket
where her chest used to be. *Lose*
something? I ask.
Your future she says and spits
five or six teeth at me.
They settle to the floor
like milkweed. A small writhing
happens vaguely under the covers.
I lean down again
and take in my arms all
that's left of her, a hint
of eucalyptus and mint, the sweetest
echo of nothing I've ever heard.

THE OPPOSITE FIELD

for my brother

I

An old photograph shows you
at two or three sitting in a puddle,
smiling, mud splattered
on your legs and shirt and face;
your arms, having swept through
the water, plunge skyward, filled,
I like to think now,
with your delight in simply being there.

Another from the same period of your life
shows you trying to drink from a garden hose,
the strong skyward arc
of water thwarting
you, your attention
immersed, your face
absolutely composed, without thirst.

In both photographs there is no future.

A figure of someone no less a stranger
emerges from these two images
the way vapor rises from Aladdin's lamp.
It takes shape, the features of its face
disposed to suggest your face, your light-
hearted summers mimicked in his gait, the crack
of the bat, sweet meat, the galling slide
into second, the earned bruise fading
into October, the mists of a possible life:

in the form this figure almost achieves
the shadows of your lost seasons call
to each other in the diamond dusk—

indecipherable voices, echoes,
and I imagine you turning in your bed
touched vaguely beneath the familiar
nightmares which have become mere aspects
of your sleep, touched so far
back, so close to what you wanted
to be, then, now,
it's as if I said *Brother,*
here we are again:

catch.

2

June, 1981. You are forty.
Il se situe par rapport au temps:
we will have to follow *that* curve to its end.

3

I had not thought to find
you so bound,
so driven into the wood.

In the sour locker rooms
we both remember—stretching
their dim tunnels from the first
wet practice all the way
to marriage—some dog
would have said *'Smatter, lost*
your balls?
            and you would have conned
him so casually, with such play—
the whole team watching—
he'd have thought you wanted
to borrow his.
                Instead,
in the thick heat of Houston,
on real grass, under a glazed dome

of sky and no one watching,
you fungo flies to your son,
to me. The thin *tick* of the wood
on the ball rehearses
itself endlessly, routine
grounder, routine pop-up, big
out *tick* routine:
after an hour
I take the bat, wave you deep
down the green reaches, stroking
them high and long, driving
you to the wall again
and again, up against it time
after time, and then *over*
the wall, Lord, into the next
field,
      farther,
           the next season,
until I don't know where
you are, have never known . . .
wanting
your will and heart to keep
from breaking—impossible—
your release into the fabulous spaces.

    4 A Lyric Meditation on Sour Locker Rooms
Almost always underground, dank,
at least one corner stinking of piss;
pasty men in cages, doling; bodies
being numbered, uniformed, strapped—
dogsbodies, dog days, even in mild April.
Can you go up
from this cavern of mock cells, single file,
into the blare of the green field,
virgin again, lined, and can you
remember how to come back down, the place
empty with you in it, alone, benched, cracked

129

in bone and will, soaked in your own sweat,
the concrete damp under your bare feet, steamed,
and no shower quite able to drown
the echoes of the metal door opening,
closing,
   the crowd stunned by the high arc
of the ball hung in the glare, against the dark.

  5
Am I brother to you
the same way I am friend
to the scattered few
people who have woven
together with me, me
and themselves: I mean, through
such distance in time
and space that the cloth
of our love seems to stretch
into transparency,
the very air of our breath,
a net so thin it may be
impossible to catch
us, no matter how far we fall?
        Hard
brotherhood.
    I prefer the sweet arc
of the batted ball, grave
and graceful at once, curving
upward and out, downward and in,
to the enfolding glove.

  6
A newer photograph shows you
and me it's not a game, this life.

The camera arrests neither motion
nor implicit gesture, you are simply

all there is, you
and the background of stones,

shadowed—your face, the lines
in your forehead. Your hair

recedes. No one needs to tell you
ghosts share your sleep.

Sometime after the shutter clicks
you probably put on your shirt,

stand up, and walk
toward home. The image

of your possible life
watches from a distance. Fading,

he picks up a pebble
and tosses it aside lightly. The sound

of its landing becomes
our purest dream.

Discovering My Daughter

Most of your life we have kept our separate places:
After I left your mother you knew an island,
Rented rooms, a slow coastal slide northward
To Boston, and, in summer, another island
Hung at the country's tip. Would you have kept going
All the way off the map, an absolute alien?

Sometimes I shiver, being almost forgetful enough
To have let that happen. We've come the longer way
Under such pressure, from one person to
Another. Our trip proves again the world is
Round, a singular island where people may come
Together, as we have, making a singular place.

This Is No Dream, This Is My Life

1

I am Humphrey Bogart.

I can do
anything.

I can take the wheel.

I can ride
the wild lust of a flame-haired woman

morning to morning,

smoke two packs
of nonfiltered cigarettes
a day,
fly.

I can
not give a damn.

I can go into my private
room, sit on the bed
and put my feet in my ears,

or sit at the window
and watch myself walk away into the mountains
forever, never
looking back,

until I am nothing
except the spoor

draining from my left heel,
following me.

Hot shit.

2

The mountains into which Humphrey Bogart
walked
are so clear this morning
it could break your heart.

Steaming slightly, his trail
could be the collected neuroses
of the Western world
since Paul's first letter to the Corinthians,
dropped finally in the chill air.

You could imagine him,
a new wind grazing his face,
done forever with the badlands
air filled with mustard and dry ice.

He might turn around near the top
and flick his cigarette toward you,
smile his enigmatic smile
as if to say *I'm all you've got*
and now I'm gone so clear

in the chill air of the morning
it could break your heart.

3

Even at this distance I can see
the pines
on the mountain where Bogey disappeared
ripple in the wind.

Empty of everything
else, I swell with such longing
I could join Macy's Thanksgiving parade
in midair, like Mighty Mouse.

Inflated thus, a growing pain,
I float out the window.
When I come to the mountains
I hover, feeling
This must be it, this must be
the one she promised
to be. And slowly come
down
into the heaving pines.

The explosion should be the end
of me, more nothing,
but instead I hear a voice
I take to be Bogey's, whispering
Leave the old bag to me
and find myself walking down
the mountain, my feet bare against the dirt,
not looking back.

from
NARCISSUS DREAMING

(1990)

THE LONG GOODBYE

Their faces are still there
on the inside of my eyelids
where I put them—
projections on a screen,
nebulae in the rich dark.
They turn toward me, turn
away. A bald, grief-slagged
head tries to dissolve
but its weight persists, forming
a pain no other shape fits.
A thin fog leaks from a corner
of its mouth, what it has left
of speech. Another with hooded eyes
swims in itself, prenatal,
the promise of its will no more
than driftwood in burred sand.
A third puts on an expression
of great knowledge it doesn't know
what to make of. It tries to smile
through all that perplexity,
becoming a lugu-
brious mo-
lecular entangle-
ment in end-over-end slow
motion, a child's hour-
glass filled with many-colored
grains of glass suspended in honey.

I sleep through them all.
In the little dark I make we are
a galaxy of affection, turning
in the sweet curves of space.

He doesn't touch
the microphone, but the way
he stands plays
on its uprightness. He is
singing about being
closer to God than ever
before, about walking
the valleys with Jesus,
about what life has
in store. His left
side between his belt
and his armpit is drawn
tight like the top
of a drawstring bag.
His denim work
shirt, forced into this small
compass, crumples
a thousandfold. His chin
drives into his left
shoulder, a fiddler
with no fiddle. His right
side is stretched
slightly—you can imagine
a bow beginning
to bend. Everything
rides on his bringing
his mouth down to the mike,
almost into it. It is more
than intimate. He delivers
his part
with such control
you hear nothing

but music, as if
he were breathing
song. When the last
harmonic fades
and the other musicians'
hands glide in slow motion
past their final
licks,
        he straightens,
disfiguring himself back
to normal, smiling
sheepishly, as if
there'd never been any good
news to bear
into the world,
to hang there singing.

AUDITION

for Darren

Nothing is
as transient as sound.
Voices
come in at the ear,
rise up in the mind.

A brief white moth
hazards its way
through foot-high corn.
A sensitive ear
follows its patterned
flight by the soft beat
its wings leave on the air.

So a song flies blind,
and the singer with it,
having only the mind's
fine trace in the ear
for his voice to follow
out to the blank air.

And then it's over. And over.
A light sleeper—
say one whose infant pain
of mucus-clogged ears
that wouldn't drain
echoes a ground beat still
under his thickening years
too deep to make flight of—

hums to himself
the white moth's

untraceable sweet
lost wake, and so mutes
his own ineffable
longing for still air.

THE NEXT STEP

If one sets aside the standard schlock
of the usual science-fiction thriller—
the sensory overload, the pseudo-shocks,
every mercenary's ideal arsenal,
and the impossible Saturday
afternoon serial cliffhanger
superchick episodes of self-rescue—
what's left?
        Well,
imagine deepest interstellar space—
the measureless, starstruck void—
incarnate as a female creature
about the size of a wholesale bargain warehouse.
She is the Causeless Cause,
the Great Egg-Layer whose endless rows
of infertile ellipsoid modules need,
in order to peel open, flowerlike, and hatch,
only a series of warm-bodies, proximate
hosts in which to clone themselves.
Hence, human intergalactic travel.
The spaceship's crew enters her
dark maw and stands upright.
They reach the murky acreage
of her ribcage and tentacled abdomen,
exploring from the inside
the Universe as Mother and Mother
Fucker in one. It's the next step
after the black widow and the praying
mantis—not to devour the male
when he's served his purpose,
but to dispense with him altogether.
A double birth, from egg and host,
and no need for a father. After the cloning

produces creature number two, the host,
in its spun glass casing, conveniently explodes.
Presumably the progeny, magnificently
dentured, go on to live forever.
                                    This is,
of course, the evil nightmare we are saved from
by the real dream that issues from it:
the macho heroine perpetuates herself
by having a daughter
without sexual intercourse, pregnancy,
labor, or nurture, discovering her instead
holed up in an air-duct complex
in the Great Mother's warehouse body
and womb, orphaned and already schooled
in cunning, independence, and survival.
She saves her
from the monstrous process noted above,
and they live happily ever after,
but not totally alone.
The extended family consists
of half an android and a one-eyed
mutilated ex-corporal who,
in an earlier reel, had taught Mom
to operate a high-tech flame
thrower and a breechsplit grenade
gun. In the end
they lay themselves down to sleep
peacefully in their cocoons of frost.

The Cabbage in History

If I stink
while I'm cooking, I'll be good
like Rasputin and limburger.
If you bury me
in the shallow earth
in a sealed crock
I will become so vile
only the delicate
gourmets of the Orient—
who also eat dog
and worship the past—
will find me
delectable. I can wrap
the ground imagination
of the Middle East in one
leaf, a gesture
as modest as God
riding into Jerusalem
on an ass. Only my cousin
the turnip shoulders
the world with less pomp,
only the onion hugs
itself more tightly. Without me
the collected sermons of Puritan
New England would have died
in the orifices of Mather,
of Edwards, odorless and
cold. Even now I am seducing
shoppers from the East
coast to the Rockies;
I boil in ten million pots.
The soft smell

of decay nuzzles Woonsocket
and Yazoo City, Eldorado
and St. Cloud, drifts lovingly
toward Melville, Alamogordo,
Cortez. No one is
safe from my implacable
aplomb, my zest.
I am headed
for the Pacific.

THE HOSPITAL OF LIES

1

My grandfather has been lying
three years in a hospital bed, diminishing.
When he is small enough
I swaddle him in a sheet, lift him
in my arms, carry him away.
I bear him along the dock
jutting into the low-tide mudflats, past
all the weeping people and people
shooting crap. They are all
swathed in white, newly
risen from their beds, immaculately
squatting in clusters in the mud.
Their dice click
against the keels of the dry boats.
Nobody looks up, everybody
watches; nobody cares,
everyone wants to take him from me.
I lay him myself
finally in the mud at the end
and sit down beside him,
waiting for the tide to come undone.

2

I sit on the floor of the hospital
where my brother is lying
over me in his newborn bed. I bide
my time, looking innocent.
My dice click against the white wall,
bounce back toward me, never
come up the same twice. I see the feet
of people who bend

over my brother and say he's beautiful.
I wait until everything else is empty,
then wrap him in a sheet
and lift him out of bed
with my claw. Scuttling, I bear him
across town, into my grandfather's garage.
While I'm hiding
us clustered in a high deep place
everyone comes together in the grease
stain spreading across the concrete floor.
All right I say, rising.
I give up; he's mine now.
I will be king and queen of the egg people
forever. Take him. I lift
his ovate body swaddled above me
and hurl it into the hard sea of people.
He should crack, he should shatter,
but he floats down and joins hands with the others.
They leave me with them
gone, again; I climb down
and sit, and watch my claw disappear
as I write my name in the grease with it.

    3

So I go into the lying hospital
my self. How else can I keep my people
from dying and being born,
from parading their don't-care
I-love-you in this muddy grease welcome
to the world? I am swaddled
in white. I lie down
and am rolled away on a table.
Wherever the others have gone
or come from will be where I am.
Whatever they have been given
to become themselves will be given

to me as well. All the people
in white will bend over me saying
We want you, we want you
gone. Hurry. There is nothing
here except everything. Take it.
Then the green men lean
over me, a black hole of rubber
closes on my face, I go backward
from 100 to absolute zero.
I forget to say this
isn't what I expected. I forget
how the king-and-queen wanted
to save his subjects and verve—
breadfather and great brother,
his killweather hardbreakers—how he wanted
to be fixed, to be perfect, so nobody
would have to be dead born dead, but

4

I wake up anyway. My grandfather
is still alive in my head
where he's been buried for thirty years.
My brother drives a cowboy Cadillac
to work in Texas, while I throw him
still toward concrete into oblivion
forty years ago now. My voice
rasps sometimes; I crave
ice cream. All the nothing
that was given back I keep
as close to me as the greasy mudtumble
I play in until I die,
as close to me as the space
left in my throat, which I talk past.

Narcissus Dreaming

He's still standing in
the boat after all
these years, his rod
angled absently outward,
the toes of one foot
nestled in an oarlock.
He might be getting ready
to step out over
the side, but there's nowhere
to go. Seems
like old times. Among the vague
ripples wrinkling
his reflection, the cork
bobs, settled
where his liquid belt
buckle shimmers, waves.
His attention all
but dissolved, the bait
long since merged
with that image the surface
keeps, suddenly
in a depth as far
from himself as he is,
something pulls. Going
through the motions
he pulls back. Bob, line,
sinker, hook return
to him, bringing
his reflection off the water
as if it were a laid-out suit
of clothes lifted
by its center. He lowers
it into the boat, takes

it upon himself,
drenched, obscene,
a perfectly imperfect fit,
leaving the water
imageless, opaque,
other.

THE HARPIST'S DREAM

The strings of her instrument become
saplings, the bark just coarse enough
to abrade her fingers as she strums.
They begin to bleed a little.
She nuzzles the roughening curve
closer into her neck, but still can reach
only the fourth tree, the rest stretching
out in a row in front of her
all the way
to the end where the mirror is.
She's down there, too, reaching
for herself. In this forest
the animals could be music
if she knew how
to make the saplings hum,
but all she gets for her effort
is more
blood. Pressing, she wants
to grow into the harp, to feel her neck
and shoulder thickening, her hair
twining upwards toward the lower
boughs, her fingers settling
into the striated rivulets of bark.
Once upon a time
she might have managed
to finish this escape—
merging with the harp trees
swaying, played by the wind—
but now she finds babies growing
on the limbs, raw, newborn
babies, bald as ice, their mouths
voiceless zeroes. One by one

she lifts her fingers to them, touching
their lips with her little blood
along the whole scale of their astonishment.
When she wakes, they begin to sing.

Umpire

for my daughter

He learns to imagine
the vertical shaft of air
hanging above home, to hear
its inaudible hum
when pitches he can't see
tick its corners.
Under the lights, when
the humidity is right, it becomes
prismatic, shimmering
with the curve's kiss,
the slider's slick dive.
Sometimes, after calling
one perfect, pivoting,
driving his right arm out
and back in a groove smooth
as a piston's, he looks away

over the green swath toward
the lights, seeming to carry
that brightness in his eyes.
If he could hold it
there all
the time no one would
argue with him,
no distorted faces writhe
Hydralike into his, no benches
clear. Everyone would see
how his vision was the strike
zone—brilliant, impeccable,

fair. And the earth is flat,
and, next spring, bull-

frogs in Bradenton will
sprout wings. Still
he lets his mind wander
briefly inside that aura,
touching the certain borders
of his calling, his peaceful dream.
Then he edges back out of it,
watches the bright air disperse,
the pitcher lean in again
for his sign.
Crouching, he rests
his hand absently
on the catcher's ribs,
feels the tender
vibrations of the ball hitting
the mitt, sensing
the red seams' rapt
nestle into the leather.
It is, after all,

the dependable magic
instant he keeps waiting
on, between the ball's
untoward rest and his own
voice breaking the silence, before
he turns the invisible
quick trace of the pitch
into a statistic, building
the box score, the record
book, some other's dream.

My Hostess at the Renovated Inn

for Tom and Shirley Ziegler

When I say her hair was alive
I don't mean to suggest Medusa.
I mean no gel or spray
had frozen the living strands
into that carvable sadness
manikins wear. It swayed.
It flowed. Put me in mind
of an underwater dancer, a dive
so deep and long breathing and drowning
become dreams of each other.
Her eyes sang, too, not a mark on them.
But you could have skated on her
apricot lip gloss, and her forearms!—
her right one lunged into a tunnel
of frisky bracelets, her left throbbed
in the coils of a brass snake.
I wanted to shake hands
for the music's sake, wanted
the apple she was, wanted to be myself
devoured, I didn't care by whom
as long as we were the whole
story.
    When she descended
the curved staircase it was no deb's
entrance. She moved
the way I dream my mother
might have moved if she hadn't been
my mother.
      She was the perfect
stranger of my heart, nameless,
moving aimlessly through the great
hall, receiving, now and then
smiling through the sheen.

When she left through the screened
door into the shadows of the porch
it seemed just right, entrance and exit,
a brilliant rift in the days'
ordinary drift and muddle, a might-have-been
as clearly marked as a fairy tale.

But as I smoothed my pants
and floated toward dinner, no more
than a customer again, she came back,
hipping the screened door open,
hoisting by one of its rungs
a ladder-backed chair like a jug
of moonshine over her left elbow,
cradling in her right arm two small
dogs, hairy, all squirm and yip.
She climbed the stairs, bumping
the ornate banister, adjusting
the dogs, rising askew along that curve
of burnished cherry, disappearing
at last, leaving a spike-heeled shoe
tilted against a riser. I stood there,
wondering if all such gifts
are inadvertent, so lonely given.
Though I seemed rooted
to the floor, and the ground
under it, my next step, going
nowhere, was curiously light.

My Children Going

It isn't even interesting.
It's the underside of the underdog
in the muck, in the end.

I tie tin cans to my tail, try
to roust the neighborhood at three
in the morning, but the streets
stay hollow—it must be the same
dream everybody's dreaming.

The music of the spheres.

Dark enough for you? a voice says.
Never seen the like of it the same voice
answers. *You can't tell
that crazy man's rattling
in your sleep from your sleep
from laughter half the time,*

can't tell it from the air I breathe.

*You ought to see somebody
about that* Perry Mason says, easing
from behind a neighbor's hedge.
He cuts through our usual nightmare
pleasantries to tell me the news
is bad. *All the sleek
anchors are melting
at their desks* he says. *What's left*

of their invented faces, hearts, drips
down their stools into the grates
in the floor beneath them. He tells me
how camera crews quit, associate
producers panic. *Under
the blitzklieg spotlights' pitiless
glare* he says *Brokaw blurs. Rather
ripples. Their thick residue clogs
the drains. The Union of Newsroom Grease
Trap Cleaners is on strike
and the studios are filling up.
Test patterns crowd the screens again,
the center cannot hold,
the season of terror is upon us.*

His lone and level voice drones lovingly
on, soothing my soul no matter what
its tragic load. I tell him
his fly's undone. *Sign of the times*
he says, turning to leave.

                                    Wait
I call to him. *What about my children?
Talk about transformation, talk
about change! Those anonymous
tadpole-shaped possibilities I flooded
their mothers with
have grown into birds
which accomplish exotic migrations
more swiftly and with less design
than light moves
on the face of the waters.*

                                  *They molt
monthly; they flash me
their iridescent names
in falling feathers. I'm up
to my knees in who they were,*

their castoff guises, not even my own
memories of them.

He doesn't listen. He lumbers off
toward reruns, toward his sequel
as Della Street's incestuous father,
the small screen rhapsody
he's always dreamed of,
bringing it all back, venting
the old office and late-night dinner
frustrations, acting out the taboos.

    3
This must be part of the real
life I promised myself some years
back, seeing them transformed
into what no one could tell
they already were
then
becoming. Gills, genes,
feathers—stranger mutations
have burgeoned in the midnight
muck, the dark dazzle
of apparent loss drawing out of itself
forward into love, walking
on air.

Hidden Meanings
for Bob Denham

Both Hansel and Jack hated their mothers:
Jack sold the old cow
so she threw his seeds away;
Hansel let his feel his fingers a lot
and then stuffed her in the oven.
Their fathers were troublesome, too:
one was a wimp willing to sacrifice
his children; the other was so big
he had to be cut down, stalk first.
We know nothing about Rumpelstiltskin's
parents, but he played by himself in the woods
and when he couldn't get a baby by proxy
stuck his wooden leg through the floor.
The two boys finally got rich, like Cinderella,
but beyond that the ends are obscure.
Maybe they entered life, and found it to be
its own magic fable, as consequential
as any *Snow White Blood Red,*
and on the surface, true.

DRESSING

About five A.M. he hears dimly
hummingbirds in the lilac, senses
the sun leaking over the slats
of cream, plays a leapfrog
of sleepandwake nobody wins
until it's too late. He'd rather
climb back down where he can
be randy Jim Dandy of the sluice
gates in spring, taking
all comers. Nothing in fact
would please him more
than to be by dreams
exhausted to deeper dreaming.
But the thin membrane between
brains fogs up like a windowpane
he could write his name on
with his finger. Only a fading
static ekes through, not even
echoes of the living life.
So it means to wake up
and put on what he does, which
he likes as one could be said
to like the melon rind after the melon,
the husk of the self.

I Can't Live Without You

I begin to die. I have been
dying all my life, of course,
but I begin
to die anyway. In my desperation
I discover a sexy woman
who wants to play. She takes
my bat and balls and fungoes me
out of the park. Flying high,
I pass the ex-poet John Keats
who has been bird hunting
and is on his way down.
John I say *this is the way to go.*
He says *When you begin to die
time is the snake woman
who loves you better than all the world.
I hate my life* he says. *I hate being
in my life.* Afterward,
I stroke her head resting
against my belly. She hums
and I feel it in my veins, my pelvis,
my throat. Our music
shimmers for old John, for our
selves, for all hearts
fluttering in their twigs of blood.

New Poems

PERCUSSION

It's nothing more than last
night's coating of ice
on the magnolia cracking
as the day rises, but it sounds
like Morse code—explicit,
measured, conversant. The tree rising
leaved among bare others
becomes isolate, too, in its own
sound, self-centered, breaking out
in a language that would invent
its listeners, the best of whom
would dance to it, hearing
the beat within the beat
sleeved, insistent. Mozart, or
the *Missa Luba.* The pupa's first
slow distending ticks
here, too, in the morning's
waste, and the wresting
of sound from the joints of a body
on the rack. The other person
standing across the lawn, just visible
through the brittle leaves, holds
his upper arm level
with the horizon, as if his elbow
were strung to a crutch above:
his neck tilts
slightly, his hand twitches. He moves
to walk, but doesn't, and his shadow
against the trunk of a bare oak seems
to do a little soft shoe.
It is a fading, brief, as the first
ice falls, and the sound begins
to diminish, and the leaves'
gloss deepens again, and warms.

THE WATER'S FINE, I'M FINE

Outlines are neither of air nor the objects
described, but, like prayer, hang between two worlds.
—Galileo

The most miraculous photograph
in the world shows my daughter
floating on her side in a lake
in central Florida. She is perhaps
three years old, most probably naked
as she was for the womb swim.
Because the photo reveals nothing
but her and the water, one can't tell
how big the lake is, or that
there are snapping turtles in it.
Although the snapping turtle has
a small brain in a small skull
it knows enough to do what it needs
to stay alive. The fetus
develops a beak called an egg tooth
it uses to break out of the first shell.
It never sees its mother, who is
gone after the hatch, but, unlike
most other animals, resembles its parents.
It's the only four-legged creature
in the world with a shell. Something else
that makes the photo incomparable
is the viscous palpability of the water:
it could have been sculpted.
Cypress trees have tanned it,
but nothing explains the irregular
striations of gray and amber
folding into each other on its surface,
as if my daughter's presence in the lens
has created a layer of life there
superimposed on the actual

water where she also floats. She is
almost laughing, the center at once
of the photographer's attention
and her own life. She could be
an invitation to her self,
or the first image of regret
that in the natural course of things
she will crawl out onto dry land.

THE EXECUTIVE DISCOVERS POETRY
for Ed Craun

He wanted to tamper,
not to intrude or repair,
but to enter the valley of this kind
of saying to see what it felt like,
or less modestly, to feel himself
drained of himself, his deepest stirring
drawn to peak and release, the sluice and pucker
of his emptying stretched to exhaustion.
He imagined lying in the stream bed
dry and panting, and mistook
that eupeptic cliché for what it's like
to enact in words the dream of consciousness.
So most men are diverted,
accepting the easy drift of the body
when the body's passing might lead to speech,
bringing hard light into the mouth of life.
So a prince might discover
a beautiful woman in the shape
of a frog, squatting beside his ledgers
and market graphs, and—instead
of kissing the swampwelted lids
of her eyes, tasting the first trickle
of his name—swallow her whole.

Coming To

for Lisa Sandlin

1

Language doesn't inhere
in anything. A label
fits on the outside, and can be
peeled off. Why else

do we say *linden*,
or *childhood*, keep our throats
primed for the next word?

A slip of the tongue can
get a man a bride, six
children, an ulcer, a life
he ends up talking to

at night when he can't hear
himself. He dreams
his words bead on his life

like water on waxed chrome,
slide off when he moves.

2

A boy sits on a stone bench
at the unspeakable edge
of two bowed lindens. His life
will inscribe an arc, fifty
years tending, until—

enovaled by a stand of trees
planted in what was ice, once,
on the bottom of the world—

he feels
the needle's point the globe spins on
touch him, and balance him,
and turn him back.

       3
He holds the secrets he has
kept from himself before
him like a microphone
with mystery at the other end,
receiving. He talks
into them, hearing
his voice recede, winding
into a dark where dark breaks.

When he listens
to his words play
back, they shimmer oddly, on
edge—a stranger talking—
as if they have gone
through something he has
no other knowledge of
and brought it back:

his life.

Love Poems

The Stars at Otorohanga

Drops of water bead
on the angel tufts. Your
raspberry breath. My hands
cradle the bright curves
of space, their drift
November's mild tray,
serving.
And here is a ladle
for the headlong rush,
the sprayed dark.
We come to this.

Butterfly

I could lift this afternoon
out of its dazed jar;
I could keep hold
of it, the elm dropping
dry leaves in July;
I could think nothing
would change
even as I peeled
the calendar of another page.
And nothing would,
does. I could keep
this kiss just an instant
from your eyelid forever.

FENCE

At first I thought she was
pounding it, trying to break out,
but her fists were relaxed
and at closer range I could see
she was holding
little felt-covered mallets, playing
a sort of tune on the corrugated steel.
She never looked my way
but anyone could tell I loved her
by the way I was
leaning into the fence,
my whole body an ear
against her music vibrating
through the cold steel. When she dis-
appeared a shimmer lifted
from the length of the fence,
a series of waves becoming sky.
I haven't stood quite by myself
since, listing one way or another,
hoping to hear the faint quiver
that sometimes does a little dance
over the beating of my heart.

His Granddaughter Arrives
for Ellen Stuart

I am a gray man leaning in a corner
but my heart sizzles with excitement,

a trapeze artist so incandescent
the ends of the earth seem
bits of string you tie on your finger
to remember by.

I have clearly done my part
in passing
on.
Who would have thought the burden
could be so easy heavy easy,

turning over and over up there—
embodiment—
until the outstretched hand
curls over the rung of the little swing
again, fits it, body
and arc of body one sweet
engagement.

Comes time.
The gray man in the corner
feels his heart go out
to her, for her,

cartwheel in the little space
it keeps up, generating to no end.

COMMENCEMENT

In the emptied stadium he leans
his back against a steel
pole beside the cinder track circling
the football field. His mother
sits at the base of the pole, on the other
side, hugging her knees.
Each of them looks through sun-
glasses into a distance.
She frowns; the hint of a shrug
forms in the muscles of her shoulders.
He feels the beginnings
of a migraine eking into the base
of his eyes. A half mile away
his daughter paces her rented rooms,
the mortarboard and robe piled
on the kitchen table. She wonders
where they are, where could they be,
the two people in separate worlds
by the pole, wondering where she is,
who's misunderstood, what to do
so they won't further lose one another.

PRESENCE

for Sid, on his retirement

Signs of the times are always disquieting,
Immanent reminders of how we're set aside,
Drawn into vacuum—a timeless bubble—where
Nothing has spread itself for us to nap on.
Even the echoes of what we knew, and how we knew it,
Yesterday, seem to disperse, and we breathe the silence.

May we hope that something can come of this

Better than the voice's fading to dry air, or

Coring inward to the commonest isolation?
Of course. Nothing is simpler. How we
Understand is everything, which we forget,
Leaving to those who come afterward
Levels to build on, soundless integuments
Insistent beneath their knowing, or unknowing.
Nobody steps aside without handing on,
Giving to time being, filling the ear with light.

LEAVETAKING
for Bob Huntley

My comfortable river
whose wide bends used to wind
aimlessly under the sycamores
suddenly stretches
into flat infinity,
a railroad track.
Eight or ten refugees
string out along it,
going no place in particular.
At night they walk the ties
as a blind person reads Braille.
Are you fertile?
a wizened crone calls.
Yes the old professor answers.
They have left
before the rising wind
razes the academies—
my old friends, going off
with their lives tied in shoeboxes
they carry under their arms.
As they hit the middle
distances, they begin to sing
the songs they've gathered into.
Their scattered rhythms
make no music I've learned
to hear, but the river
bends again, and the sycamores
rustle and bow;
their bark resembles
the spotted skin of old people.
They seem to be the source
of a light that breaks

into the air above them,
where the voices of the lost
finders rise. There's no way
I can follow them, I haven't
gone so far, but what they leave
me keeps. I see them begin
to fade almost
before the first bend
obscures them. I wave, stirring
the thin air I can't breathe
deeply enough.

LOVE'S BODY

I kneel beside her,
touching my fingertip
to a vein: at once
a heartbeat and the want
of life. The little
pool at the back
of my mind
ripples a second
skin, my breathing,

the edge of everything.
The air thins;
around my brittle
tinder—the surface
of heat my body
is—it is full
of unlikeness.
              Through
the membrane of the pool's
declining a bird lifts,
the eye of time, fledged,
dripping with aspiration.
It spins slowly upward,
suspends itself. If it flies

it is in my turning,
the planet's turning,
and does not appear
as something I see, append.
It has troubled

to stir, and rise,
commend itself to air,
my self to air:
                    heartfire
and the end of longing.

THE WRITING MACHINE

I sleep in it.
It's a cross between an iron lung
and an incubator, varying in size
according to my fear of being seen.
It affords me no physical
nourishment or warmth.
It's like a Sabbath
in that it enables worship
but isn't an object of it.
Its light
helps me to read fine print
at two hundred feet, depth or distance,
and to figure out which of the world's
rejection slips are love letters.
I accumulate a rhythm
in its body similar to the heart's
beat in mine, complete with tics
and pauses: I hear it telling
how loss dies into sweetness, dies
into the next mouth that will speak
its living. I hear it lodge
the stone in the jackal's throat.
Yet in spite of every appearance
I know it does nothing
but enclose me, a spun self.
Without it I would never wake up.

Light Years

His life started
as an anecdote,
a kite with a tail
to fly in the small winds.
Who would believe it?
He began to talk
to himself, which meant
he had to invent
a self to talk with.
Two kites dipped
together in the sky.
They made their own
currents of air
in the air. If the words
don't slide through
a tunnel they make
into the void, where
do they go? He knew.
He knew who was
listening. He could see
the sweet slipstreams
of the kites designing
themselves from themselves.
He knew also he wouldn't
go on forever. The secret
was to keep
beginning without losing
it all, or losing
the beginning in it all.
Light was the rest
of the secret, as in keeping
a light hold on the strings.

However long, it was
a story
quick in the telling,
made up of air
and the resistance to air.
At the precise
instant the kites faded
into their woven patterns
a sudden brightness spun
down the strings
through him into the ground,
leaving a life rooted,
uplifted, spreading
into a place for birds
to light, and sing.

The questionable old man wanders
the refuse dump, the railroad yards,
in his head, deserted, gets out of bed,
traverses the room, goes down the stairs,
his pajama shirttail flapping,
the thin cotton pressing his legs.
Look at that shin—razor sharp:
barefoot to the wind, no more regard.
I meet him coming
out of the front door at midnight.
He points his finger at the moon,
pulls the trigger. I ask him
where he's going. *Off* he says.
The upstairs bedroom sucks at him
through its open window, a vacuum cleaner;
his hair flows toward it. He lifts
his arms, grabs a low branch of the maple,
hauls himself up. Moonbird,
limbnestle. The tree vibrates
from the suction. At its top finally,
he hooks his toes into the ruff,
flaps his arms, flies with the tree
his wake, gone. The bedroom window
shudders, a mouth moaning.
I sit down in the great rootgap
his takeoff has left me, his will,
hoping to die in such arms.

SPELL

for Chris Wiman

DREAM

He wants to dance in the grave
so he digs it thirty-six feet square—
an admirable hole,
an impeccable hole.
Because he has dug it,
he is in it, the continuing
beginning of his life
where he will bury his saving.

HIS MOTHER'S HOMETOWN

The river's mouth
his mother's hometown skirted

emptied its whole width
at low tide,

leaving bare to the slow sky
its common bed.

Rank, scrawled debris
dotted the black purview:

sunken tires, rubbers, dry
shells bleached to the last hue

of fragility.
Even the least shy

sordid bottom creatures withdrew.
It seemed a bare depth

Where the already dead came to die.

THE CLASSROOM

A voice told him decades ago
he wasn't shoveling these words around
searching for happiness.
So many lightlaced phrases
absorbed by the yellowing earth,
so many people gone.

Risen?

It seemed unlikely,
but with his head bowed
toward the jigsaw verbal
light he choreographed with
light down
here who
could tell?

Why else
did this
        miraculous
hole stay
        empty—

giving it all away
in the immense loss
gone in the earth

light dancing
graveroom well?

Was it his grandmother cancer
who had in his infancy
language said

Pray

tell?